PENGUIN BOOKS

My Little Black Book:
A Blacktionary

T0096534

My Little Black Book:
A Blacktionary

The pocket guide
to the language of race

**JANE OREMOSU AND
DR MAGGIE SEMPLE, OBE**

PENGUIN BOOKS

PENGUIN BOOKS

UK | USA | Canada | Ireland | Australia
India | New Zealand | South Africa

Penguin Books is part of the Penguin Random House group
of companies whose addresses can be found at
global.penguinrandomhouse.com

Penguin
Random House
UK

Published in Penguin Books 2023
002

Copyright © Maggie Semple and Jane Oremosu, 2023

The moral rights of the authors have been asserted

Typeset in Georgia Pro Regular 8.5/13 by Jouve (UK), Milton Keynes
Printed and bound in Great Britain by Clays Ltd, Elcograf S.p.A.

The authorised representative in the EEA is Penguin Random House Ireland,
Morrison Chambers, 32 Nassau Street, Dublin D02 YH68

A CIP catalogue record for this book is available from the British Library

ISBN: 978-1-804-94230-7

www.greenpenguin.co.uk

Introduction

We have always been fascinated by how people speak and act. A driving force behind our work is the belief that interpreting words and seeking their meaning from a linguistic and non-linguistic perspective can help each of us make sense of the world. It is said that the English vocabulary has over one million words in it and that we use relatively few of them. Words are constantly changing in the way that they are spelled, how they are pronounced and what they mean. Some words are no longer used, as they have become outdated or may well be offensive. So what do you do when language changes, especially when it is the emotionally charged language of race?

In recent years this was a question we were often asked in our work as thought innovators and change agents. People wanted to discover how to know what was right and what was wrong, where to go and how to keep up with the fast-moving pace of the language of race. We became curious and investigated further. Our curiosity gave rise to research, many conversations with others, finding out their views and thoughts. The result? That, if there is one thing people from all different backgrounds can agree on, it is that it's difficult to know, to find out, to be sure what is acceptable today and what is not. This guide is a first step towards clarity, with a focus on Blackness.

Writing this book came in response to organisations looking for support in navigating the language of race. Many of us use words without really knowing too much about them. We wrote this book to help everyone further their own knowledge and understanding; to have a starting point for further conversations. The goal of this book is to encourage and enable more people to become comfortable having uncomfortable conversations in an ever-changing environment. It is also a way to remove the excuse 'I don't know how to'. We know it takes courage to admit that help is needed and even more to have conversations around race. What better way than a pocket-sized Blacktionary to help get these discussions going.

The aims of this book go beyond helping you to be PC (politically correct) or no longer having that young person in your family tell you that you are out of date for saying a certain word. Ntozake Shange, playwright and poet, once said, 'I'm a firm believer that language and how we use language determines how we act, and how we act then determines our lives and other people's lives.' *My Little Black Book* operates with the premise that most people want to be considerate and to live in harmony with others, particularly those who are different from themselves; to be respectfully curious to broaden their own knowledge and experience.

Language plays a key role in one's sense of belonging and feelings of safety. It is the way by which people communicate with one another, build relationships and create a sense of community. Everyone wants to be 'seen, heard and understood'. How we feel and, therefore, respond is largely determined by our interactions with each other and the environments we immerse ourselves in. But language is not just external; we all have an internal dialogue and our interactions with each other impact that internal self-conversation.

Making a conscious decision to raise awareness of our internal and external narrative allows us to be deliberate in the way we communicate, be it with words or through our behaviour. *My Little Black Book* provides historical insights, societal context, reflective thoughts and actions to take as well as definitions of words. You will see in this book words that are loaded with meaning, and that they are placed within a context. We hope that the examples of how and when to use certain words or phrases, as well as some tips to consider, will be useful.

The purpose of this book is to provide a starting point for conversations off the page. You will learn things, but remember your learning doesn't stop at the back cover. There is digital content available, you can meet us at our road shows and, of course, we welcome your comments. We hope you enjoy the process and use this book as a springboard to be brave and talk to family, friends and colleagues about it too.

The Authors

Born in the UK and moving to Nigeria at the age of five with her Nigerian father, English mother and brother, Jane lived her formative to young adult years in Lagos. Her father always said to her, 'You can do anything you want once you get your first degree.' She took this literally, and once she graduated she booked a one-way ticket back to the UK at the age of twenty-four. Excited about beginning a new adventure in the country of her birth, Jane arrived in London full of zappiness, only to have a rude awakening when a racial slur was directed at her. In Nigeria, since everyone is Black, no one really is, so this experience awoke within her a sense that being Black was not acceptable, and that people would judge her by the way she looked first. She described it as a shock to the fabric of her belief system, a realisation that she needed to code-switch to fit in, in order to succeed and therefore survive.

Jane went on to hold various leadership roles in global organisations for a period of twenty-two years. In late 2017 Jane had a life experience that transformed her forever. She embarked on a journey that was to change the course of her direction, challenge her values and belief system and break down the self-imposed barriers. She decided to leave the corporate world to follow her passion and today runs two businesses, one of which is I-Cubed Group.

She dedicates this book to her son, Akintunde.

ABOUT MAGGIE

As a child, Maggie could be found in the Arthur Simpson Library in Crouch End, London, where she grew up. At home she was surrounded by books and people visiting, and by debates about Black people in the UK. Her parents taught her about racism and the meaning of words and actions. They encouraged her to follow her dreams.

After attending school and university in England, Maggie worked in the public and private sectors. She became an academic and began advising governments in the mid-1990s, and has been a member of several high-profile UK Government and European Union task groups.

In 2004 Maggie established a global consultancy firm to provide strategic advice on business ethics, leadership, equity & inclusion, cultural change and board development to international companies. She established a fashion brand in 2010 that designs and produces bespoke women's clothing.

Maggie serves on a range of Boards. She is a Non-Executive Director of Phoenix Holdings Group plc; Jamaica National Bank UK Ltd; and a member of the University of Cambridge HR Committee. She was awarded an OBE in 2001, is cited in *International Who's Who*, is an Honorary Bencher of Middle Temple and a Fellow of the City and Guilds Institute.

Maggie's dedication goes to all of the brave but quiet Black people who went before her as agents of change.

Accent Bias

Making judgements about people who speak a language based on their accent and, in particular, discriminating against people with an accent different from that of the dominant culture.

Accents form a large part of our identity and are one of the ways we express ourselves as individuals. They are developed when we learn to speak and are heavily influenced by the people around us during our early years, the movies we watch, who we listen to and other elements of our environment. Accents tell people where we might be from, for example: our place of origin, what our native tongue might be and which social groups we may identify with. Everyone has an accent; it is not unique or unusual.

Noticing an accent different to our own is second nature. However, when we act more favourably to people who speak and sound like us, bias is in play. Judging people on how they sound instead of their value can lead to inaccurate and unfair decisions being made. This can be in the form of perceived capability, intelligence, pain thresholds, earning potential and educational achievement. Individuals affected therefore try to change their accent to be accepted. This is not sustainable and can lead to exhaustion and stress, as rejecting a person's accent also rejects their identity.

In the workplace employers rarely consider accent bias a form of discrimination. Many state that they are an equal opportunity employer and that all applicants, both internal and external, will be considered for roles. An equal opportunity employer pays attention to the nine protected characteristics (age, disability, gender assignment, marriage and civil partnership, pregnancy and maternity, race, religion or belief, sex and sexual orientation) when assessing an applicant to ensure fairness.

A better understanding of the role accent plays in our (often inaccurate) appraisal of individuals and groups facilitates greater acceptance and lessens our discriminatory attitudes and behaviour. Here are a few ways to get started:

1. Acknowledge that we all have an accent; include accent bias training as part of your organisation's on-boarding.
2. Train all employees on what accent bias means and how it shows up.
3. Actively stand up for those who are called out for their accents.
4. Practise speaking words from a country you are visiting where English is not the first language to get a feel of your accent in another language.

Adultification of Black Children

When Black children are viewed and treated as older than they are by adults who are in positions of authority, resulting in their rights being violated, diminished or ignored.

The term adultification refers to a young person who has had to grow up before their time. When used to describe Black children, it explains a form of racial discrimination where they are perceived as adults even though they are not. Systemic racism has forced them into social, emotional and physical adult roles before they are ready. It is becoming more commonly used as a term in the UK in recent years, having originated in the USA in 2008.

Three major incidents happened in the UK in 2022–2023:

1. Child Q, a twelve-year-old Black girl, was strip-searched by police at school, while menstruating, without an appropriate adult present.
2. Two Black brothers aged thirteen and fifteen were at a station in Bromley where one forgot their train pass. Excessive and physical force was used on the fifteen-year-old by four male adults, including holding his neck and forcing it towards a wall.
3. In 2023 a Black teenage boy aged fifteen was wrestled to the ground and handcuffed in a well-known pharmacy by two privately employed civilian security staff.

In these examples the Black children were treated as though they had more agency and capacity to safeguard themselves. They were treated as mature and resilient. All Black children are at risk of this type of discrimination, which has extremely damaging effects. 'Adultification can also impact children mentally due to missing out on formative milestones in adolescence, it can harm their ability to make and maintain healthy relationships with others,' Sharnade George, psychotherapist and Founder of Cultureminds Therapy, explains. 'Not being seen as the child you are can make you feel less than, which in turn can impact you emotionally, physically and mentally, making you feel ignored and disregarded. In the long term this can lead to depression, anxiety, low self-esteem and trauma, as their innocence and vulnerability is erased.'

Affinity Bias

The tendency for people to relate to others who share similar interests, experiences and backgrounds (also known as 'similarity bias' or 'similar-to-me' bias).

American sociologist William Sumner articulated the behaviours associated with 'similar-to-me' bias. He observed how people were inclined to treat others much better when they were part of their in-group. We define an in-group as a group of people with common values and interests, producing a sense of belonging and feelings of solidarity. Years later, Henri Tajfel, a Polish social psychologist, conducted a series of experiments in the 1970s and early 1980s that demonstrated that even an arbitrary allocation of people (for example, by the toss of a coin) to different groups caused 'us and them' distinctions and triggered in-group bias. He concluded that the ability for humans to form a strong sense of self is largely dependent on their group memberships. This suggests that we show favouritism towards people who we see as similar to ourselves, as our collective identity aids in the construction of our individual identity. When we meet new people, we automatically look for similarities, which is instinctual and linked to our survival mode. We feel 'safer' with those who look like us, sound like us, have similar interests and backgrounds.

Affinity bias is common during the hiring process in workplaces. This 'similar to me' effect is subtle and passes under the radar unless there is a high level of self-awareness. It might manifest itself, for instance, as thinking that someone is qualified for a role because they have worked in similar companies to us, have the same outside interests or attended the same university. We make assumptions about their skills, abilities and overall conduct, placing them in a more positive light. It subsequently leads to unconscious discrimination against those who are different to us.

While similarities shouldn't automatically disqualify a potential candidate, being aware of them will help with making objective hiring decisions. Here are some steps you can take to avoid affinity bias in the workplace:

1. Be aware of the language you use when writing job descriptions. Avoid making them too prescriptive.
2. Anonymise the CVs of applicants.
3. Have a diverse interview panel.
4. Look for experiences, skills and uniqueness.
5. Use a strength-based framework (asking applicants about what they love to do) together with a competency-based framework (exploring what applicants can do).
6. Adopt a 'culture add' approach, where new employees bring innovative ideas, life experiences and different perspectives to help an organisation grow and evolve (rather than a 'culture fit' approach where new employees have to fit in to an existing culture).

Affirmative Action

A series of policies that aims to increase the opportunities provided to underrepresented members of society.

Affirmative action is from the United States and came into practice in the 1960s, a time of significant social and political change. The Civil Rights Act of 1964 and the Voting Rights Act of 1965 were landmark pieces of legislation that aimed to end racial discrimination in a number of areas such as voting, education and employment.

While affirmative action is not part of UK legislation, other countries such as Canada, Brazil, South Africa and India do have laws around this policy.

Afro

A hyphenated term to describe something that is said to originate from Africa.

The prefix Afro derives, along with its variants, from Latin and it relates to ethnic origin, meaning native to Africa or African. Originally the Latin word was used only in reference to the region around modern Tunisia, but it was gradually extended to the whole continent. Today it is a word-forming element and has been used to prefix words to describe links to Africa or to signify that its roots originate in Africa, for example: Afro-visible or Afro-hairstyle.

Including the prefix Afro to denote the nationality of Black people across the world creates a sense of pride and belonging. It promotes unity between Black people and brings a sense of recognition and unspoken acknowledgement of the history and struggles shared across generations.

Afrocentrism

An approach to the study of world history that is centred or focused on the continent and countries of Africa and its people, especially in relation to historical or cultural influence.

The term originates from African-American scholars such as Molefi Kete Asante, professor and philosopher, in response to the dominance of eurocentrism. (Eurocentrism is the assumption that European culture, history, values and achievements are more important than any other cultural reference points.) He maintained that Africans had been moved off-centre in terms of identity, culture, and history. In other words, they had shifted away from their own perspectives by having been influenced by European culture.

Afrocentrism seeks to place Africans at the centre of their own narratives. It defines a worldview that is delivered from an African perspective where Blackness is not suppressed or concealed, and the influence and importance of African contributions are a focus of examination and emphasis. Now, Afrocentrism is becoming more of a movement than a historic position. Knowing the historical and cultural influence of your heritage plays a crucial part in feelings of pride and self-worth. We are noticing that narratives of Black lives are being re-centred and are no longer governed by Europeans. The emerging momentum associated with decolonisation leans heavily on Afrocentrism. An example of this is decolonising the educational curriculum in schools to ensure that the literature studied is curated from a wider perspective. Another example would be understanding that art from the African continent has influenced the world more widely.

Afro Descendent

A shortened term that refers to a person of African descent.

A person who is of African descent but was not born or is not living in an African country. Normally a descendant of an enslaved ancestor shipped to the Americas via the Atlantic Slave Trade between the sixteenth and nineteenth centuries. The term can also be used to refer to the descendants of North Africans who emigrated to other parts of the world.

The modern African diaspora consists of millions of people of African descent living in various societies who are united by a past based significantly, but not exclusively, upon slavery and racial oppression and the struggles against it. They share an emotional bond with one another and with their ancestral continent of Africa. Regardless of their location, they face broadly similar problems of racism and discrimination, economic inequality, health disparities and cultural appropriation.

Afrofuturism

A cultural aesthetic, philosophy of science and history that explores the developing intersection of African diasporic culture with technology.

Afrofuturism looks forward. The term was coined in 1993 by culture critic Mark Dery in his essay 'Black to the Future'. It evaluates the past and future to create better conditions for present generations of Black people through the use of technology, often presented through film, art, music and literature.

Afrofuturism is an expansive term encompassing a whole movement of art, philosophy, activism and more from across the African diaspora. It imagines a future free of racism and oppression of Black communities and gives hope by providing a platform where Black people thrive in their own culture, imagining themselves achieving greatness while operating under their own positive influences. It is the story of musicians, artists, writers, philosophers, fashion icons, filmmakers, costume and set designers, actors, activists and academics who believe in a better future for Black people and for all people.

The Afrofuturism movement is now recognised as a powerful creative force that dares to imagine a world where African-descended peoples and their cultures play a central role in the creation of that world. With certain power structures still in existence that prevent young Black people from realising their full potential, this movement provides a visual of what a truly inclusive future looks like and inspires many to continue to believe in its possibility. It provides hope for a bright future.

While it is most commonly associated with science fiction, Afrofuturistic works can also be fantasy, alternate history and magic realism. *Black Panther* and *Wakanda Forever* are two examples of films that can be described as Afrofuturistic.

Afro Hairstyle

Natural hair that Black people comb out into a style.

The hairstyle is referred to as an 'Afro' because most people who can grow one have Black African heritage. In ancient African societies, hair was a sacred cultural and spiritual symbol as it was thought to be a source of personal and spiritual power. In the 1950s and 1960s, the civil rights movement sparked a change in the way Black people viewed themselves and their hair. Prominent civil rights activist Angela Davis was one of the first women to wear her Afro during this time and inspired many women to do the same. The Afro was much more than a hairstyle; it became an incredibly powerful political symbol of the movement. It is a symbol of survival, resistance and celebration. Black people were embracing who they were and their Afro hairstyles became a reflection of the pride they had in their African heritage. It signified freedom, self-acceptance and natural beauty and depicts the journey many Black people have endured to be self-expressive. In the 1970s, the Afro comb was worn in Afro hair as a political emblem and a signature of a collective identity. It was recognised as a symbol of comradeship and of saying no to oppression.

Today, there is a natural hair revival for many Black British people; they are embracing the way their hair grows and its natural textures. Many were inspired by former First Lady Michelle Obama in 2017, who was seen wearing her natural hair once she had left the White House. Not long after this #naturalhair was trending on social media platforms, with many Black women making the decision to unapologetically wear their hair naturally. In 2017, Michelle De Leon created World Afro Day, which is an annual celebration of Afro hair celebrated worldwide on 15 September each year. It has been described as a global day of change, celebration and education and is endorsed by the UN Office of the High Commissioner for Human Rights.

We call our Afro hair 'the crown of glory' and Black people stand tall because of it. For those of you curious but not bold enough to ask, let's help out. Firstly, there is a truth about Black people and the relationship they have with their hair. While hair means something different to each of us, being Black with Afro-textured hair has a uniquely meaningful history. Secondly, Afro-textured hair can be changed to feel and look different depending on preferences and occasions, and the beauty is that it can be changed again and again. In other words, Afro hair can be worn in many styles. There is also a sense of pride and strength that comes with sporting an Afro as it adds to the confidence of our self-image. It is usually the first thing people see as it has its own energy and essence. It is an expression of being Black and a symbol of self-love. The bigger the better! Lastly, whether at home or in hair salons, the styling of hair involves storytelling and the sharing of views, bringing Black people together.

When our hair is touched without permission it is a violation of our personal space and boundaries, and it is inappropriate and disrespectful.

Afropean

A person of African descent living in Europe who is juggling their multiple allegiances and forging a new identity.

The term Afropean was coined by David Byrne, the Talking Heads singer, to describe the music of Zap Mama, a group founded by Marie Daulne, who was the daughter of a Belgian father and a Congolese mother. Their album *Adventures in Afropea* was released in September 1993 and presented a blend of European and African musical styles, which was unique at the time. The term Afropean was used initially in artistic circles as a way of describing the African influence on European culture. In 2019 Johny Pitts, the author of *Afropean: Notes from Black Europe*, explored 'Black Europe from the streets up' in his book. He writes: 'The term Afropean encouraged me to think of myself as whole and unhyphenated' and sees it as something that Black people may feel more comfortable with in the future, as being a more accurate fit than being described as an African immigrant.

Today, the word Afropean refers to those who are part of the Black diaspora living in Europe and is a celebration of the coming together of African and European styles and influences. Many Black people have made the European continent their home and are creating a new identity.

Afro Visible

Embracing positive, beautiful images of Afro hairstyle (see page 16).

Black people, and especially Black women, have been on a journey when it comes to embracing their natural hair, from changing the texture to adopting Western hairstyles. This has been driven by the need to fit in, to make others feel comfortable and to be accepted. Now Black people are breaking the mould by returning to their roots, literally and metaphorically. This act of accepting one's beauty and presenting our true self as we are is extremely liberating.

Being visible, seen and accepted with our natural hair in all walks of life is fast becoming the norm. The Afro hairstyle is big and it's bold, it grows out and not down, it's easy and comfortable to manage and a symbol of pride for a Black person. Seeing Black people in public spaces embracing and proudly wearing their Afros is inspiring to the next generation.

Ally/Allyship

An individual who actively speaks out against discrimination and stands up for a person or group that is being discriminated against or treated unfairly. An ally challenges themself, their own behaviours and the behaviours of those around them.

Allies are individuals who have made a conscious decision to inform and raise their level of awareness by listening, asking questions, increasing their knowledge and recognising the part they have played in unfair systems. They are open-minded to exploring the struggles that minority groups have had to face. Being an ally is a life-long process and involves understanding one's own privilege, using it to make decisions and act in the knowledge that it will change oppressive systems. This can be uncomfortable at times and may include taking risks.

The term gained popularity in the 2010s and has grown since the murder of George Floyd in May 2020. Interest in allyship in the workplace rose significantly after May 2020 as organisations wanted to make a difference. The aim was to consciously create an inclusive environment where people felt safe to be their authentic selves. They have also been deliberate in their supplier selection process and the awarding of contracts, with the intention of growing the Black business sector.

The great thing about being an ally for one group of people is that it can open our eyes to being an ally for everyone. People don't fit into just one box, so we have to be intersectional (see page 85) if we want to do it well. We can be allies wherever we go, for example: in the workplace, volunteering at events, in our social circles, when networking, on social media platforms, as a parent, with our parents. Let's make it part of who we are for the good of all.

There is a thin line between showing you want to make a change and being a true ally. Performative allyship is a form of virtue signalling (see page 131), which is a practice of gestures that do more to promote an individual's own virtuous image than help marginalised people. Disingenuous behaviour within an organisation can lead to tokenism (see page 124), detrimentally affect inclusion efforts and diminish the support of the race equality agenda, to name a few side effects. Ultimately it can affect the health and safety of Black people and their quality of life.

Consider the following ways to become a true ally and see which work for you:

1. Listen to what people are saying from Black communities, face to face or via social media channels.
2. Read books and educate yourself, family and friends on relevant topics.
3. Speak up when you see or hear injustice happening around you.
4. Become a diversity & inclusion champion in the workplace.
5. Welcome your own discomfort and explore the reasons for it.

Anti-Racism / Anti-Racist

A person, policy or practice that actively opposes racism and promotes racial tolerance.

Not being racist and being anti-racist are not the same thing. Non-racist (see page 103) is passive behaviour and unknowingly complicit. Anti-racism is about action; action to identify and to eliminate racism in order to transform the world. Ibram X. Kendi, an American author, professor and leading scholar on anti-racism, believes that denial is at the heart of racism. Becoming anti-racist requires quiet reflection, and careful and critical examination of belief systems, habits and actions. It involves actively changing thoughts, feelings, beliefs and behaviours at the individual, institutional and structural levels, and deliberately raising one's awareness of how race and racism affect Black people. It is the act of understanding the complex and varying ways in which racism operates across all walks of life and committing to be part of its eradication.

There has been a rebirth of anti-racism activity due to the murder of George Floyd in May 2020. It is no longer acceptable to be complacent or uninvolved in the eradication of racism. Many organisations have taken an introspective approach, looking at their people, culture, policies, procedures and systems and changing actions and behaviours to demonstrate their anti-racist support. This tragedy engaged and accelerated organisations to act in a way not seen before.

Becoming aware of unconscious biases (see page 128) that exist within ourselves and society, educating yourself and others and not placing the responsibility on Black people to do the work are a few examples of how to be anti-racist. Here are some steps you can take:

1. Understand the difference between being non-racist vs anti-racist.
2. Be observant and identify racial inequalities around you in everyday life – what do they look and sound like?
3. Have open conversations with your family about what anti-racism means for you.
4. Champion anti-racist ideas.
5. Be comfortable with feeling uncomfortable for a while.
6. Hold friends and family accountable.
7. Have and hold intentional conversations with peers and colleagues.

8. Avoid stereotyping and the use of microaggressions and call them out when you see other people doing them.

Anti-Slavery

Opposed to the practice or system of slavery.

British abolitionists actively opposed the trans-Atlantic trade of African people from the 1770s, however it took until 1833 for the Slavery Abolition Act to come into effect as an Act of Parliament. It cost the British government £20 million to buy the freedom of enslaved people at the time (approx. £20 billion today). This debt, paid off by the British taxpayers, did not go to the enslaved people, but instead went to compensate the slave owners for their loss of 'property'. Even though this payment was made, supposedly freed enslaved people were committed to up to twelve more years of further service to slave owners. It wasn't until 1838 that this agreement was abolished.

The loans taken out to fund the payment were only just paid off in 2015, according to the UK Treasury. Shocking as this may sound, it explains why the collective energy around slavery still lingers today. Between 10 to 12 million Africans were transported across the Atlantic between the sixteenth and nineteenth centuries. Historians estimated that between 1.5 million to 4 million died aboard slave ships during the crossings, and this number does not include those who died while trekking sometimes up to 300 miles across land to the ships.

Although slavery was abolished over 200 years ago there are constant reminders of slavery in UK society today. These are in the form of statues, names of streets, schools and buildings, plaques and other memorials. The toppling of the statue of Edward Colston, a major Bristol slave trader, during the UK Black Lives Matter protests in 2020, questioned and brought to public attention the tributes to slave owners by local authorities and institutions.

Attribution Bias

The tendency to explain and judge a person's behaviour (often incorrectly) by referring to their character rather than any situational factor, based on prior observations and interactions with other people.

Psychologist Fritz Heider first discussed attributions in his 1958 book, *The Psychology of Interpersonal Relations*. He noted that people tend to make distinctions between behaviours that are caused by personal disposition versus environmental or situational conditions. He also predicted that people are more likely to explain others' behaviour in terms of dispositional factors (i.e. caused by a given person's personality), while ignoring the surrounding situational demands.

The main characteristic of attribution bias is perceptual error which then leads to biased interpretations and decision making. An example is the perceptual error of the 'angry Black woman'. This stereotype characterises Black women as aggressive, hostile and overbearing. When some people see a Black woman become upset or angry, they're more likely to attribute the emotion to her personality instead of to the situation that caused it. This erroneous conclusion could lead to poor treatment and a lack of empathy, particularly in the workplace.

Having to suppress and hide emotions for fear of being stereotyped creates a lack of trust and builds walls. Putting yourself in another's shoes is one way to help combat this. Responding with empathy and understanding before arriving at a conclusion will help break down these negative stereotypes. Here are some ways to combat attribution bias:

1. Practice self-awareness – recognise you have attribution bias and when it occurs.
2. Challenge your internal stories and dialogue.
3. Ask questions, focus on the objective facts.
4. Listen with the intent to understand.
5. Avoid blaming others.

B

BAME

Black, Asian & Minority Ethnic. A term initially used for data gathering that has turned into a controversial acronym to describe people who are not White.

A controversial acronym that groups diverse communities together, which is not helpful for understanding the differences between these communities. BAME implies that members of these communities share the same experiences and face the same challenges, when in fact they don't. Grouping diverse communities together under one term risks the erasure of individual identities and experiences. This term is now outdated.

BBVP

Black British Voices Project, initiated by Maggie Semple as a result of her belief that the contemporary views of Black British people had yet to be understood.

The project investigates the evolution of Black British identities with the aim of providing an updated portrait of Black Britishness for the twenty-first century. The national survey was launched on 24 May 2021 by I-Cubed Group Ltd, University of Cambridge and *The Voice* newspaper. The lead researcher is Dr Kenny Monrose, Fellow of Wolfson College, University of Cambridge. Of the 11,000 respondents, more than half were women aged over forty-five.

The question that the survey wanted to find the answer to was: What does it really mean to be Black in Britain today? There were five key themes that emerged:

1. Identity – What is 'Britishness'?
2. Building a life – young people and the future;
3. Well-being – mental and physical health;
4. Challenges – criminal justice system; media, arts and sports;
5. Wealth & representation – financial capacity, business and enterprise, politics.

Belonging

The feeling of relatedness or connection to others that is easy and non-judgemental and provides a positive impact.

Belonging is the feeling of acceptance, demonstrated through treatment and support received wherever we go. It is when we can be our authentic selves without fear of negative judgements and/or repercussions.

We all like to belong to groups, be they social, familial or professional. It's an instinctive human need. Belonging increases our rate of survival and is crucial to our life satisfaction, happiness, mental and physical health and even longevity. It gives us a sense of purpose and meaning. When we don't feel like we belong, it can lead to feeling lonely and isolated and has long-term implications for mental health. A study published by *HR Review* in September 2022 noted that a staggering 42 per cent of UK employees do not feel a sense of belonging at work.

A workplace culture of belonging creates an environment that provides comfort, connection and encourages full contributions. It is no longer enough to just appreciate the role undertaken; we want our uniqueness to be celebrated and encouraged. A quote, often attributed to Vernā Myers, an American diversity and inclusion advocate, author, and speaker, says: 'Diversity is being invited to the party, Inclusion is being asked to dance and Belonging is dancing like nobody's watching, because that's how free you feel to be yourself.'

When an individual feels like they belong at work, it influences how they contribute with ideas and creative thoughts. This has a positive impact on business performance as well as the employee's overall well-being. One study conducted by BetterUP found that employees who feel a strong sense of belonging are 18 per cent more likely to stay with their organisation, seven times more likely to feel engaged at work, and three and a half times more likely to contribute to their fullest potential. The research also found that UK employees with a lower sense of belonging are 80 per cent more likely to quit their jobs. For Black people a lack of belonging results in feeling insecure about their place in the organisation, which then impacts their overall performance and may lead to apathy and even their resignation.

Measuring belonging through confidential, third-party employee surveys can encourage employees to share open and honest feedback about their experience in the workplace.

Bias

The action, treatment, inclination or prejudice for or against one person or group, especially in a way that is considered to be unfair.

There are many different types and guises of bias towards Black people.

We explore the following in this book:

Black British

A term that Black people who are culturally tied to Britain may use to describe themselves.

Black communities have been present in Britain since at least 1500, and during the 1750s London became the home of many Black people.

The term Black British was developed in the 1950s. It refers firstly to Black British people from the former British colonies in the Caribbean, today called the Windrush generation by some (and who are widely viewed as being pivotal in the rebuilding of post-war Britain); secondly to people from Africa, who are residents of the United Kingdom and are British.

The Black population in the UK today accounts for approximately 3 per cent of the national total and equates to around 2 million people. According to the 2021 UK Census, those identifying as Black British in England & Wales numbered 2,409,278 or 4 per cent of the population.

The Black British Voices Project (see BBVP on page 27), the first survey of its kind and with record numbers completing it, explored the contemporary views of Black British people in 2021. The project investigates the evolution of Black British identities with the aim of providing an updated portrait of Black Britishness for the 21st Century.

Black Consciousness

A mindset and way of life for Black people who know their potential and value.

The term Black consciousness was originally used by the American educator and civil rights activist W. E. B. Du Bois. He said that people of African origin should take pride in their Blackness. In the 1960s Steve Biko, a South African anti-apartheid activist, pioneered the philosophy of Black Consciousness as a movement. The movement sought to raise Black self-awareness and to unite Black students, professionals and intellectuals. It also motivated many Black people to confront not only the legal but also the cultural and psychological realities of apartheid, seeking real Black participation in society and in political struggles.

Black consciousness remains a defining feature of Black writing in Britain. In 2020 there was great interest from readers of all different backgrounds to gain knowledge of issues about race and racism. Bookshops were inundated with a sudden release of published books by Black writers. That same year Candice Carty-Williams and Bernardine Evaristo, both Black female authors, won awards at the British Book Awards – Book of the Year and Author of the Year respectively. Reni Eddo-Lodge, another Black female author, topped the paperback non-fiction chart.

Black Cultural Identity

A person's self-concept and self-perception relating to a social group that has its own distinct culture.

Our identity is what defines us as human beings, but most of us don't really think about what it actually is. Cultural identity is developed from identification with a culture and a sense of belonging to a particular group. It plays an important role in an individual's sense of self and how we therefore relate to others. Language is a fundamental aspect of cultural identity and it has been said that culture and identity are first formed when we learn to speak.

Cultural identities include a broad set of constructs related to demographic sub-groups such as ethnicity, gender, race, sexual orientation and socio-economic status, to name a few. It is important, however, not to confuse Black identity with Black culture or communities, as there are many different Black cultures.

Embracing our cultural identity can help us feel more satisfied, more connected to our sense of self and in our relationships and give us more confidence in who we are. Have you ever thought about what shapes your cultural identity? How does your behaviour display who you are as a person? What do your clothes or attitude say about you? How do the experiences you enjoy describe you?

Black Energy

A collective aura from Black people that inspires others to take action and create positive social change.

A collective positive aura is the overall vibe of a group that has come together with good intentions that are greater than the sum of their parts. This leads to a sense of unity and harmony, creating a ripple effect that extends beyond the group. An example would be the Black Lives Matter (see page 36) movement where people all over the world united to advocate for change and the common goal of creating a more just and equitable world.

Black Excellence

Celebrating the achievements and success of members of Black communities.

The term Black Excellence was originally coined in the USA during the civil rights movement. Its purpose was to amplify the voices of shunned Black communities who were striving to make a difference. Black Excellence has two schools of thought depending on one's perspective. The first is celebrating and upholding Black communities and their achievements while acknowledging the challenges these communities face. The second is the pressure felt by having to constantly strive for excellence and the impact this can have on the well-being of individuals.

It is a mindset and a determination to be outstanding in one's achievements, ability and success as a Black person. Saying someone or something exudes Black Excellence is an acknowledgment to Black people who have already done extraordinary things or who have sacrificed so that others could be positioned to do so. Representation is also important and Black Excellence elevates it greatly by inspiring the next generation. In the UK today there are more and more events celebrating Black Excellence: The Black British Business Awards, Black

British Theatre Awards, MOBO Awards, The Powerlist Black Excellence Awards and London Chambers Black Excellence Awards are a few.

We have to be conscious of having a balance, as in recent years the concept of people who are considered to exhibit Black Excellence often face unreasonably high expectations and standards, especially when held up as representatives of the entire Black population. In this way, anything less than excellence or perfection may be viewed as failure, creating an impossible standard.

Black Fatigue

The exhaustion felt, resulting from experiencing and/or combating small acts of aggression and disrespect that a Black person experiences day to day, combined with the endless need to prove one's worth. (See Emotional Labour on page 66.)

Black History Month

An annual observance originating in the United States in 1969, where it is also known as African American History Month. It has received official recognition from governments across the world (February in the USA, October in UK).

Black History Month in the UK was organised through the leadership of Akyaaba Addai-Sebo, a Ghanaian analyst and activist, who was working as the Special Projects Officer at the Greater London Council (GLC) at the time. He wanted to mark the contributions of Black people in the UK, so planned and discussed with his colleagues at GLC a way to do this. He collaborated, coordinated and held the first official Black History Month event on 1 October 1987.

It began as a way of remembering important people and events in the history of the African diaspora. Now Black History Month is an opportunity to start conversations about Black cultures that are informative, educational and supportive. Each year has a different theme to focus on throughout the month. In the UK you'll find everything from great historical discussions to food festivals to music workshops to seminars and lectures to fashion events and plenty more. These events celebrating African and Caribbean cultures and histories run for the whole month until 31 October.

Black Identity

A person who understands what it means to be Black and the history of their heritage.

Black identity refers to the complex and multifaceted sense of self and group belonging of individuals who identify as Black. This identity can encompass various aspects of a person's life, including their cultural, historical and social connections to the African diaspora, as well as their experiences with discrimination, racism and systemic oppression. Black identity can also be shaped by external factors such as family, community, education and media representation. It is an important and powerful aspect of Black people's lives, and has been celebrated and explored through various forms of art, literature, music and activism.

Black Lives Matter

The collective description of the condemnation of the unjust killings of Black people by police and the demand that society value the lives and humanity of Black people as much as it values the lives and humanity of White people.

In 2013 three Black women, Alicia Garza, Patrisse Cullors and Opal Tometi, created a Black-centred political movement called #BlackLivesMatter in the USA. It was in response to the acquittal of George Zimmerman, who was charged with the murder of Trayvon Martin, a Black teenage boy in Florida.

The organisation raises awareness of ongoing injustices towards Black people to bring about meaningful change.

Black Mixed Race

A term that categorises and makes the assumption (based on the colour of a person's skin) that one of their parents is Black. It is becoming an outdated term. (See Dual Heritage on page 64.)

Black Pound

The economic spending power that all Black people collectively have.

Recognised as holding a powerful position in the retail market, driving trends across food, beauty, media and more. Predictions say this influence will continue to grow as buying power grows and is projected to reach $1.8 trillion in the USA by 2024. This has been put down to the increase in numbers of the US Black population, on track to grow by 22 per cent (NielsonIQ).

While the majority of research around Black spending power is on African Americans based in the USA, there has been a growing recognition of the economic agency of Black people in the UK. Some businesses have begun to tailor their marketing and product offerings to appeal to Black consumers, recognising their unique cultural preferences.

We are becoming increasingly socially conscious, spending deliberately and carefully, choosing to support businesses that have a positive impact on the world around them. Today's generation of Black influencers are quick to use social media platforms to show support for brands and retailers that reflect their values. They are highly digital, more brand aware, very clear on their values and unafraid to share their thoughts and opinions on what is, and is not, acceptable. Their span of influence is far and wide and has retailers and manufacturers now paying attention to what drives Black people to make a purchase.

If you are part of an organisation that sells a product or a service, ask yourself:

- How do you attract Black spending power into your organisation?
- What values do you represent that aid or hinder this?
- How many Black-owned businesses are on your supplier list?

- What percentage of your spend is with Black-owned businesses?

Blackfishing

A term for the action where an individual who is not Black appears to be Black for financial or social rewards.

The term was coined in November 2018 by journalist Wanna Thompson, after she saw a Twitter discussion about White women cosplaying as Black women. She said, 'Blackfishing is an issue because it allows a person to pick and choose the "cool" parts of being black, without facing any of the discrimination that black people do. Black is cool, unless you're actually black.' Examples of Blackfishing include: tanning or darkening the skin, adopting Black hairstyles like Afros, braids or cornrows, use of Black-style lyrics and gestures in music and music videos, use of implants, injections and fillers to enhance parts of the body to embody Black features.

Blackfishing is seen as a type of interpersonal racism that depicts Black people as a stereotype and Black culture as a product. Those who engage in it commodify the Black experience for profit. Influencers and celebrities are known to pick which features they deem attractive and adopt them for financial gain, greater influence and/or popularity.

Non-Black people profiting from a culture that has been historically discriminated against for years, without actually experiencing the disadvantages and oppression associated with being Black, is harmful to Black people. Beyond feeling stressed, disrespected, and tired, Black people might also experience depression or anger after seeing Blackfishing take place.

Blackism

An ideology, mindset and positive movement promoting Black people.

Blackism seeks to re-establish and reaffirm the primacy, identity and personality of Black people. It advocates an acceptance of Afrocentrism (see page 13) and unity.

Blacktionary

A glossary of terms and phrases to aid racial literacy with regards to the language of Black race.

Blacktionary, a play on the word dictionary, explores a range of definitions related to the language of race. The first edition of *My Little Black Book, A Blacktionary* was published in October 2021 by Jane Oremosu and Dr Maggie Semple OBE as a response to UK-based organisations looking for support on how to have conversations with their Black employees in the aftermath of the tragic death of George Floyd in May 2020. It originally contained the definitions of 100 words, many of which are included in this version.

Blacktivist

An activist for the Black diaspora.

A term that combines Black and activist to describe anyone who actively promotes change for the benefit of Black people. A Blacktivist would work to address systemic racism, inequality and injustice by being an ally (see page 19). They also work to promote Black cultural expression and celebrate Black history and achievements.

C

Code-Switching

Adjusting one's style of speech, appearance, behaviour and expression in ways that will optimise the comfort of others in exchange for fair treatment.

Adjusting ourselves to different situations is something that most of us do unconsciously. Much depends on the dominant culture which may be explicitly or implicitly stated. Think about a time when you were in a social setting and you felt that the topic of conversation made you feel uncomfortable. Initially, you probably showed interest by nodding or making the odd comment in agreement, but what you really wanted to do was speak out. This is an example of code-switching and we all do it.

However, for some people code-switching isn't a once-in-a-while technique but a regular way of life. Many Black people will be used to code-switching and do so by trying to 'fit in', hoping that by making others feel comfortable, they will be treated more fairly. In a workplace environment, we may feel the need to dial down our accent, alter the way we dress, change our hairstyle or hide tattoos in order to progress professionally.

In November 2019 *Harvard Business Review* published an article identifying the main reasons why Black people code-switch: downplaying membership in a stigmatised racial group helps increase the likelihood of being hired and seen as a leader; and expressing a shared interest with members of the dominant group raises the chance of promotions.

Yet code-switching comes at a huge psychological cost as it involves changing behaviour, predominantly toning down a part or parts of one's personality, and it takes a toll on those who feel the need to constantly monitor themselves, what they are saying, what they are doing or how they are behaving. Being vigilant of one's mannerisms is exhausting and ultimately results in burnout, mental health issues and emotional stress.

Consider meeting with individuals who you have observed code-switching at work and have an open and frank discussion about it. Identify clear actions that can be put in place to minimise this, for example:

1. Identify ways to educate yourself on what code-switching looks like at work.
2. Create a safe place and environment so Black employees have a voice at the table without fear of recrimination.
3. Encourage senior leaders to champion authenticity at work.
4. Have a 'come to work as your authentic self' day each week or month.
5. Plan activities that encourage everyone to engage during Black History Month.

Colonialism

A practice of control by one group of people or power over another group of other people, by establishing colonies and with the aim of economic dominance. In the process of colonisation, colonisers impose their religion, language, economics and other cultural practices on the oppressed group.

Colonialism occurs when one nation subjugates and overpowers another by force, manipulation or coercion and establishes satellite colonies that are often governed remotely. Resistance and instability are inherent by-products of colonialism, often resulting in ethnic-based conflicts backed by colonisers who have gone on to develop hierarchal structures of preference of one ethnic group over another. Colonisation changes names of locations, destroys borders by annexation and alters religious/spiritual practices and customs without consultation or consent, and can even recalibrate language and replace cuisine and gastronomy.

Colonialism is as old as civilisation itself, dating back to Mesopotamia and antiquity, and has played a significant role in human history. From the sixteenth to the nineteenth centuries enslavement was a form of colonialism that had a devastating impact on African people, from the first invasions led by the Portuguese and Spanish before other European nations such as the British, French, Dutch and Belgians also became involved.

Maritime and trade partnerships were an established part of the so-called scramble for Africa, where the continent was divided amongst European nations for the acquisition of resources and economic control. This also included the installation of their own cultural practices, human rights standards, medicine and parliamentary processes, whilst simultaneously disregarding indigenous cultural norms. Further to this, indigenous peoples were excluded from decision making and governmental procedures.

The consequences of colonialism are still being felt today. It is evident how long-lasting the legacy is in terms of the perception and treatment of Black people. Many Black people have been conditioned by colonisers to feel a denial and shame around their indigenous culture and identity, which has been passed on to following generations.

Colour Blind

A denial of thought when seeing someone's skin colour, especially when it's Black, and being unaware of the challenges that come with it.

Colour blindness in relation to skin colour is an untruth. The brain is designed to seek out differences in order to identify an immediate threat to guarantee survival. It is a basic human instinct. Unless an individual is sight impaired everyone sees the colour of a person's skin. Saying we don't see colour infers a lack of awareness, dismisses lived experiences, ignores inequities and minimises the need for conversations around racism.

We found in our research that many well-intentioned people say, 'I don't see colour, I just see people.' Have you ever said this and asked yourself why you say this? Are you aware of any reactions when you do? Perhaps you're trying to be inclusive and helpful; however, in reality it ostracises those affected. Not having one's skin colour acknowledged implies only chosen parts of a person are 'seen' and not the whole person. Invalidation of heritage, experiences and cultural differences occur when this happens.

Racial colour blindness creates an immediate lack of trust and an instant alertness in the individual who experiences it. Can you remember a time when you felt invisible? For example, in a meeting where your idea was taken by someone else who presented it as their own? Or perhaps in a virtual setting where you kept raising your hand but were not invited to speak? Did you find your attention divided between how you were feeling and being fully present? These internal sensations of discomfort are similar to those who experience the denial of the colour of their skin.

Colour Brave

Unafraid to have candid conversations about race that help better understand other perspectives and experiences.

Coined in 2014 by Mellody Hobson at her TED Talk titled 'Colour Blind or Colour Brave', she describes colour brave as recognising the importance of acknowledging the reality that we all see colour. We are observant, we take note of the people around us, purposefully and intentionally. Having real conversations about race can be uncomfortable and even awkward. How do we move past this? Our journey has to begin with introspection; let's identify our narratives and beliefs about race. To be colour brave we need to raise our awareness around our own thought processes and internal dialogue. Equipping ourselves to have these conversations will also help us change others' views and perspectives. We need to learn how to become colour brave; it is a decision and an action.

Ask yourself, who can you have a conversation about race with: a family member, a trusted friend? What are each of your perspectives? What triggers come up?

Colour Consciousness (also Colour Observant)

The opposite of being colour blind (see page 44). Seeing, accepting and acknowledging the challenges that arise with being Black.

Colourism

The practice of favouring lighter skin over darker skin.

Colourism was a device used by European colonists to create division between enslaved Africans and further the idea that being as close to White as possible was the ideal image.

Today it remains a form of discrimination with devastating effects. It hasn't helped that the beauty industry has created skin lightening products that bleach the skin. In June 2020, Black British singer Alexandra Burke spoke of how people in the music industry had told her to bleach her skin in order to succeed. That same year, Black British musical artist Beverley Knight told ITV News that the music industry is keen 'to market people who are perhaps a little lighter than I am because it's seen as being more mass accepted.'

Communities

Social units that group people together.

While Black people appear to share common characteristics, they have many differences and should not be referred to singularly as the Black community. Black people belong to diverse communities with different cultural backgrounds and experiences. Their experiences and cultures are shaped by a variety of influences such as language, religion and tradition.

Confirmation Bias

The tendency to interpret new evidence as confirmation of one's existing beliefs or theories.

Confirmation bias can also be described as an error in thinking. Our brains are designed to take shortcuts. When we are presented with multiple facts, which appear time-consuming and energy sapping, our brain selects the information that agrees most with our pre-existing knowledge. These mental shortcuts employ a practical method that is not guaranteed to be optimal, perfect or rational, but is nevertheless sufficient for reaching an immediate, short-term goal or approximation. One of the most common examples of confirmation bias is how we seek out or interpret news stories. We are more likely to believe a story if it confirms our pre-existing views, even if the evidence presented is shaky or inconclusive.

Confirmation bias has serious implications for Black people as it leads individuals to select bits of information that reinforce prejudices or stereotypes. The evidence is in the treatment of Black people by the justice system, in health care, education, at work, in the sporting world and across all aspects of life. This inability to seek objective facts can result in bad decision-making and poor judgements.

To rule out exclusiveness and embrace inclusiveness we need to retrain our brains to work better for us. Slowing down allows us to challenge our existing thoughts. Although confirmation bias cannot be entirely eliminated, here are some ways to overcome it:

1. Accept that confirmation bias exists in all of us.
2. Research fully when searching for information and actively consider all the evidence available, rather than just the evidence confirming your belief or opinion.
3. Change systems and processes, not individuals.
4. Slow down and act deliberately.
5. Collect and analyse data on diversity within your organisation.
6. Seek the opinion of others when you know it differs from your own.

Critical Race Theory

The core idea that race is a social construct, and that it is not merely the product of individual bias or prejudice but also something embedded in legal systems and policies.

We all possess a lens through which we see the world and the many factors that form our lives. Critical Race Theory (CRT) is such a lens, and is an approach that helps us observe and examine race and patterns of racial inequality. CRT asserts that racism exists within all daily interactions, both cerebrally and physically, and uses the intersections of social variables to demonstrate the pervasive nature of racism. It acknowledges that the legacy of slavery, segregation and the imposition of second-class citizenship on Black people and other people of colour continue to permeate the social fabric of nations. CRT recognises that race intersects with other identities, including sexuality, gender identity, socioeconomic status and others.

CRT emerged in the 1970s after questions of race were raised following the cessation of the American civil rights movement. This was an interrogation led by legal scholars from Harvard Law School such as Derrick Bell (the first Black Professor of Law at Harvard) and other activists as an attempt to address the subtle forms of racism that were ubiquitous within legislation. The origins of the term CRT is attributed to Kimberlie Crenshaw and builds upon four significant movements and theoretical positions. These are: standpoint epistemology, radical feminism, critical legal studies and the Black Power movement.

The application of CRT remains a challenging pursuit and we see CRT receive backlash from both sides of the political divide.

The political right inaccurately suggests that CRT presupposes that all White people are racist and, as a result, attempts to shut down debates of racial inequalities; and, on the other hand, the political left suggests that CRT removes the focus on class position and economic disparities, which many see as the most significant determinants of social inequalities.

Cultural Appreciation

When someone seeks to understand and learn about another culture to broaden their perspective and connect with others cross-culturally.

Appreciation can also be seen as a cultural exchange of sorts. Cultural harmony is achieved through knowledge and respect of different cultures. Exchange, sharing something about yourself, learning something about someone else and participating in a mutual understanding of one another's background and culture are all deemed appreciation.

It involves a keen interest and genuine, sincere curiosity in wanting to learn about another culture different to our own. It's about sharing knowledge, ways of life, differences, ideas. For instance, this could look like being a traveller not a tourist when visiting other countries, reading literature from another culture, watching a film in another language with subtitles, participating in cultural practices like traditional dances or cooking classes and learning another language. Other examples include:

1. Appreciating and sharing the culture being celebrated by wearing culturally appropriate clothing at a celebrated event;

2. Openly communicating the origin and history of the custom or item that you are embracing;
3. Giving recognition to the culture you are choosing to appreciate by having conversations;
4. Giving credit where it is due and questioning the background of the item when making new purchases from different cultures.

Cultural Appropriation

The inappropriate or unacknowledged adoption of elements of one culture or identity by members of another culture or identity, often for economic reward or for social kudos.

Cultural appropriation can include exploitation of another culture's religious and cultural traditions, hair, style of clothes, dance, art, symbols, jewellery, aesthetics, values, language, food and music for personal gain or interest. Cultural elements that may have deep meaning to one culture may be diminished by those from another culture. Instead of honouring another culture, appropriation demeans and dishonours. It perpetuates harmful stereotypes and deepens divides between communities.

Some examples of appropriation include:

1. Taking a photo of a ritual ceremony and posting it on social media for the sake of getting likes;
2. Going to a music festival wearing a costume that imitates another culture with the intention of getting attention or likes on social media;
3. Mimicking a person's accent under the guise of humour.

Appreciation - Appropriation: what is the difference?

This is a question that is often asked. Cultural appreciation can very easily turn into cultural appropriation.

A fine line separates the two and it is a continuous learning journey that we are all still navigating. Experiencing another culture doesn't automatically mean we understand it or that we should take elements of that culture and claim them as our own. It's important we understand that sharing and taking are two very different things.

Where do we draw the line between 'appropriate' forms of a given culture and more damaging patterns of cultural appropriation? We have all experienced people crossing that line at times, and the important thing is to keep talking about it and constantly learning. We encourage you to continue exploring to bring increased awareness and clarity to this topic, as it is not a conversation that many people have regularly.

A good starting point is to ask yourself:

1. What defines culture?
2. What might make up culture for a group of people?
3. What might inform other people's decisions to make a cultural choice that could be seen as offensive?

Here are some suggestions on how to take part in another culture without exploiting it:

1. Examine and reflect on your own culture. Is it central to your identity and would you be offended if someone were to use a certain aspect of it without fully understanding what it means?
2. Listen to stories being told to get a better understanding of other cultures.

3. Consider context – what does a certain symbol mean to a particular culture? Inform yourself about the origin of the item.
4. Share your own culture in return.
5. Cultivate and maintain an attitude of sensitivity.
6. Recognise and embrace cultural differences.

Cultural Competence

A set of values, behaviours, attitudes and practices that come together within a system, organisation or among individuals that enables them to work effectively in cross-cultural situations.

Achieving cultural competence is a dynamic, ongoing developmental process that requires a long-term commitment from everyone. It's the ability to honour, understand, communicate with and effectively interact with people across cultures. It involves respecting beliefs, language, interpersonal styles and behaviours. Without cultural competence, our opportunity to build cross-cultural relationships is impossible. Instead, we'll co-exist with people we don't understand, creating a higher risk for misunderstandings, hurt feelings and bias.

On an individual level, cultural competence is an examination of one's own attitude and values, and the acquisition of the values, knowledge, skills and attributes that will allow you to work appropriately in cross-cultural situations. At a systems, organisational or programme level, cultural competence requires a comprehensive and coordinated plan that includes policymaking, development of infrastructures, delivery of services, enabling support and programme administration and evaluation.

Developing cultural competence consists of four building components: knowledge, awareness, lived realities and skills;

two supporting skills: cultural intelligence and emotional intelligence; and three capabilities: intercultural teamwork, conflict management and cultural desire.

A culturally competent person demonstrates the knowledge, skills, attitude and behaviour to work and communicate effectively with others from diverse cultural backgrounds.

Here are some of their characteristics:

1. An awareness and understanding of their own cultural identity and biases;
2. A willingness to adapt and adjust their behaviour and communication style to easily interact with those from diverse backgrounds;
3. An ability to identify and address cultural stereotypes and cultural barriers to enhance effective communication or understanding;
4. Having respect for the diversity of others and their cultural backgrounds;
5. Showing sensitivity to the potential impact of cultural differences on interactions and relationships.

A culturally competent organisation would recognise, encourage, promote and support these qualities.

Here are some ways to become more culturally competent:

1. Engage in cultural appreciation (see page 50).
2. Be conscious of the dynamics inherent when cultures interact.
3. Value diversity and similarities among all peoples.
4. Understand and effectively respond to cultural differences.
5. Engage in cultural self-assessment at an individual and organisational level.

6. Make adaptations to the delivery of services and enabling support.
7. Institutionalise cultural knowledge.

Cultural Diversity

Appreciating the existence of a variety of diverse and different cultures within a society.

Cultural Intelligence (CQ)

Refers to a state of mind in which a person understands and navigates different cultural situations effectively.

Cultural intelligence is developing the skill to relate and work effectively in culturally diverse situations. It's the capability to cross boundaries and prosper in multiple cultures.

The world is becoming an increasingly global community. Individuals who possess high levels of cultural intelligence play an important role in bridging divides and knowledge gaps both inside and outside of the workplace. It is a very valuable social skill and one that can be learned. With an ability to relate to others with empathy and understanding, cultural intelligence is often linked to emotional intelligence. People with emotional intelligence pick up on the emotions and feelings of others. People with cultural intelligence attune to the values, beliefs and styles of communication of those from different cultures. Businesses that don't practise cultural intelligence may find themselves falling behind as customers and employees favour businesses that provide this type of experience.

One example of a cultural intelligence framework is the four-factor model of cultural intelligence developed by Christopher Earley and Soon Ang. This model identifies four key factors that contribute to an individual's ability to function effectively in culturally diverse situations:

1. Cognitive CQ – the ability to understand cultural differences and similarities in thought, communication and behaviour;
2. Physical CQ – the ability to adapt to different physical environments such as food, climate and housing;
3. Emotional CQ – the ability to be aware of and manage one's emotions in cross-cultural interactions;
4. Behavioural CQ – the ability to modify one's actions and communication style in a culturally appropriate way.

Cultural Competency – Cultural Intelligence: what is the difference?

While both of these terms relate to the ability to work effectively with individuals from diverse cultural backgrounds, they differ in their focus and approach:

- Cultural competency focuses on developing knowledge and awareness of cultural differences and then applies that knowledge to work effectively with individuals from diverse cultural backgrounds.
- Cultural intelligence, on the other hand, focuses on developing skills and strategies for adapting to diverse cultural contexts. It is the ability to adjust communication and behaviour.

Cultural Vibration

A powerful sensation felt as a result of a collective achievement or injustice.

The collective psychological impact of a traumatic event witnessed in real time, watched or heard about, on a group of people can translate into damaging mental health and physical effects. An example of cultural vibration happened in 2020 with the death of George Floyd. The feelings surrounding this injustice were felt collectively, and especially in Black communities. An online article published by *Stanford News* in the USA over a year later highlighted the psychological impact of his murder. It showed that, immediately after Floyd's death, feelings of anger and sadness increased. Nearly one in two Black Americans reported feelings of anger (48 per cent), representing a two-fold increase from the week before. Sadness also soared, with 47 per cent of Black Americans reporting feelings of loss, despair and grief.

'Seeing a member of one's group killed engenders a feeling of threat and vulnerability,' said Eichstaedt, who also directs Stanford's Computational Psychology and Well-Being Lab. 'It touches the emotional core of who we are.'

D

Decolonisation

Refers to the action or process of undoing the effects of colonisation.

The decolonisation movement gained momentum after the Second World War and saw a number of Black nations gaining so-called independence well into the 1980s. However, the current uneven development of the global south (regions within Latin America, Asia, Africa, Oceania) is evidence that colonialism still exists, disguised as international development. We still see many countries being monitored and controlled. This is visibly marked by currency iconography and the theft and removal of art, historical artefacts and treasures to European vaults, private collections and museums.

In recent times, artefacts and art works that were stolen are being returned to their country of origin by a number of European museums, including the British Museum.

Diaspora

Those who identify with a homeland but live outside of it.

The term defines the dispersal of a group with a common heritage and symbolic values that attaches them to a particular landmass. Diaspora communities represent and maintain a culture different to those of the countries within which they are located, often retaining strong ties with their country and culture of origin (real or perceived) and with other communities of the same origin.

The etymology of the term diaspora is rooted in the Greek translation of the Hebrew Scriptures 'dia sperio', meaning to sow over or scatter. This was a term used exclusively and associated with Jewish history until the twentieth century. During the 1950s and '60s anthropologists began to apply the term to the human displacement and global movement of people, for example sub-Saharan Africans who were removed from their homeland due to the transatlantic slave trade. Historically this has been impelled by the mechanisms of empire, imperialism and or colonialism.

In recent years the usage of the term has shifted to include broader definitions. For example, it is now used in modern debates surrounding refugees and voluntary migration, transnational relationships and international development. The concept of diaspora is undergoing a process of transformation from simply a dispersion of people to the formation of an identity in a different part of the world. Its negative connotation is being replaced by the realisation of its positive outcomes, such as the impact on the economic development of the country of origin by promoting trade and direct foreign investment, creating businesses and spurring entrepreneurship, as well as transferring new knowledge and skills.

Digital Blackface

Describes the act of non-Black people who produce, post or circulate 'Black reaction' GIFs online and especially on social media threads to express various emotional reactions.

To understand digital blackface, we must first understand the concept of 'blackface', which is the inherently racist practice of performing a caricature of a Black person by a non-Black person, typically White individuals, to entertain an audience.

This racist practice has sadly entered the age of the internet. The term was coined by Joshua Lumpkin Green in his 2006 Master's thesis – *Digital Blackface: The Repackaging of the Black Masculine Image* – and refers to 'the way in which technology allows non-Black people to "try out" Black identities online'. It has been described as the commodification of Black people on social media by non-Black individuals, and takes many forms, including but not limited to: using memes, videos, photos, or GIFs – even those that are funny, celebratory or seemingly innocuous – featuring Black people, and using darker emoji skin colours that are not reflective of the person's skin colour.

Taking responsibility for what we post and why is the first natural step to preventing digital blackfacing. Let's be mindful of the ways different races are represented in the images and GIFs we choose to use on social media. Do they uplift or drag down? Outrightly avoiding digital blackface should be our ultimate aim. It's not about not showing Black images at all; it's about being mindful of the way Black people are represented and ensuring there are no further harmful or stereotypical representations of any group of people.

Digital blackface gives non-Black people a false understanding of how Black people exist in the world. Here are a few ways to avoid it:

1. Inform and educate yourself and all digital and communication staff about digital blackface.
2. Consider if the images you've chosen to post are reflective of the communities your organisation serves.
3. Before you post a meme, image, GIF or other visual media, think about whether or not the image reinforces stereotypes.

4. If you are unsure about whether or not an image, text, video or GIF perpetrates digital blackface, don't post it.

5. Discuss any questionable tweets, stories, or posts with others – sometimes, having more than one pair of eyes on something helps evaluate potentially problematic content.

6. Do your own research, listen, seek out information and think critically.

Digital Whitewashing

The lack of digital representation for Black people when wanting to use an emoji or emoticon as an expression of communication that is reflective of their skin tone.

A picture paints a thousand words and is a great form of expression. Communicating with the use of emojis and emoticons is one of the ways we identify and self-represent online. Skin tone modifiers are a vital part of how users construct their online identity. In 2015 five extra skin tones were added to emojis, which was great progress towards digital representation. Yet picking the right emoji to convey exactly what you are feeling as a Black person can still be difficult due to the lack of variety in skin tones across all the emojis available. There just aren't enough.

There is a correlation between how users see themselves in their relationships with others online and their sense of self-worth. We all want to be able to represent ourselves correctly. Have you ever stopped to think about the things you take for granted? Look at your phone and look at the emoticons. What do you notice? For example, many of the emoticons are coloured yellow and we have to personalise them to reflect our identity. What about the virtual meeting environment? Have you noticed how many apps embrace and include the option to personalise? Can you imagine if all the emoticons were black as the default format?

Discrimination

Treating a person or a particular group of people differently, especially in a negative way, from other people.

Discrimination occurs when a person is unable to enjoy their human rights or other legal rights on an equal basis with others because of an unjustified distinction made in policy, law or treatment.

Black people experience discrimination in a range of contexts and forms. One example is in the workplace during the hiring process, promotions or pay discussions. This can include a Black person being passed over for a role or promotion in favour of a less qualified non-Black person.

Many organisations are proactively looking at ways to combat discrimination in the workplace, and a good example is the reporting of the ethnicity pay gap.

Diversity

The range of human differences.

Diversity is what makes each of us unique. It includes our backgrounds, personality, life experiences and beliefs, all of the things that make us who we are. It is a combination of our differences that shape our view of the world, our perspective and our approach.

In the UK there is a growing awareness of the benefits of greater diversity. An example is representation in the media, with more diverse characters and storylines being featured in TV shows, movies, advertising and social media. Another is in the workplace, where many organisations are promoting diversity by creating an inclusive culture through their recruitment processes, raising awareness and in reviewing their policies and practices.

Dual Heritage

A preferred term used by some Black people who have one parent of Black heritage, replacing Biracial and Black Mixed Race (see page 36) as a form of description of identity.

As race is a social construct, referring to an individual as being of two or more races is outdated and restrictive today. The majority of people in the world have ancestral links to different heritages that add to the wonderful tapestry of who they are. A feeling of global unity and oneness is starting to override what once was a feeling of separation, and the term global majority (see page 76) is being used more frequently.

E

Emotional Labour

The effort that a Black person applies in order to regulate their emotions and expressions for the comfort of others. (See also Black Fatigue on page 34.)

The effort expended to regulate emotions is a daily occurrence for Black people. Examples include: the pressure felt to educate others about issues related to race and racism, having to constantly navigate and negotiate racist systems and frequent experiences of microaggressions (see page 96) and discrimination (see page 63).

Entreprenoir

A visionary and innovative Black person who has an idea and creates a product or service that people will buy.

A celebratory and positive term that denotes Black role models across society. They generate wealth, provide work opportunities for others, have a social media presence and give back to their communities.

Equal Privileges

Where skin colour does not play a part in the treatment received.

A concept where being Black does not inform decision-making processes or choices made, but is acknowledged. Individuals are granted the same rights, opportunities and access to resources without discrimination (see page 63). When Black people feel that they have the same privileges as others, it fosters a sense of inclusion.

Ways to adopt this behaviour include:

1. Treating everyone with respect and fairness regardless of their skin colour;
2. Evaluating people based on their qualifications and abilities;
3. Being open to different perspectives and willing to learn from others;
4. Engaging in meaningful discussions and taking action to promote racial equity.

Equality

The state of being equal, especially in status, rights or opportunities where each individual or group of people is given the same resources or opportunities.

The UK Equalities Act became law in 2010 and covers everyone in Britain. It protects people from discrimination, harassment and victimisation in employment. It has three main purposes – to eliminate discrimination, advance equality of opportunity and foster good relations between different people when carrying out their activities. The characteristics that are protected by the Equality Act 2010 are: age, disability, gender reassignment, marriage and civil partnership, pregnancy and maternity, race, religion or belief, sex and sexual orientation.

Equity

The quality of being fair and impartial. It recognises that each person has different circumstances and allocates the exact resources and opportunities needed to reach an equal outcome.

Equity was added to the language of diversity and inclusion in 2015, with the aim of not just levelling the access, but also the opportunities presented, promoting fair treatment while working to eliminate institutional and unconscious barriers. Today, many organisations have policies and behavioural guides that are underpinned by an ethos of equality, but as diversity and inclusion work developed, it became apparent that opportunities were not fair to all.

Equity recognises that not everyone is starting from the same base. A great way to visualise what equity looks like is by looking at a family of four purchasing bicycles. Equality says that all four have the same size bicycle. Equity, on the other hand, says the children need smaller bicycles so they can reach the pedals because they are shorter in height, while the adults need bigger bikes because they have longer legs and can reach the pedals more easily.

How will someone who has never had the opportunity to lead a team be able to apply for a role that requires this experience? A recruiter that understands equity will ensure that 'leading a team' can be evidenced in many ways, such as leading a staff network. Or how can someone be promoted to be a leader if they have never been given the opportunity to display their leadership skills? Knowing this, a recruitment panel may decide to hire on potential and show equity in this way.

If you lead or co-ordinate any type of group, think about how you manage the dynamics of who gets to do what. Do you demonstrate an understanding of equity? Would others describe you as equitable?

Equity – Equality: what is the difference?

Equity is often confused with equality, however equality doesn't necessarily achieve the same outcomes as equity, so what is the difference? Equality means each individual or group of people is given the same resources or opportunities. Equity recognises that each individual or group of people has different circumstances and allocates the exact resources and opportunities needed to reach an equal outcome.

Ethnicity

A grouping of people who identify and share with each other a common cultural, historical or ancestral heritage that distinguishes them from other groups.

Ethnic groups may share a narrow or broad spectrum of genetic ancestry, depending on group identification, with many groups having mixed genetic ancestry. It can be an inherited or societally imposed construct not necessarily based on shared genes or DNA. Ethnicity tends to be defined by a shared ancestry, language, history, culture, religion and common sets of tradition. Ethnic groups can be broadly or narrowly construed: for example, people in Great Britain can be considered British or more specifically English, Scottish or Welsh.

Here are a few ways to embrace different ethnic groups:

1. Understand how culture influences people in terms of behaviour, beliefs, and values.

2. Be aware of your own cultural conditioning.
3. Be considerate, sensitive and respectful of other cultural and other religious beliefs and practices.
4. Respect differences in perspectives.
5. Avoid stereotyping.
6. Read broadly. Beautifully written prose allows us to step into someone else's shoes, even if only momentarily.
7. Choose media wisely. With web surfing and media streaming, the world is just a click away.
8. Try something new.

Race – Ethnicity: what is the difference?

Race describes physical traits, while ethnicity refers to cultural identification. Race is identified as something you inherit, whereas ethnicity is something you learn. Race refers to dividing people into groups, often based on physical characteristics. Ethnicity refers to the cultural expression and identification of people of different geographic regions, including their customs, history, language and religion. Race is determined by how you look, while ethnicity is based on the social and cultural groups you belong to.

Ethnocentrism

Seeing one's own culture as the correct frame of reference and way of living.

Ethnocentrism refers to judging other groups from our own cultural point of view. Individuals who are ethnocentric tend to have negative attitudes towards other cultures, believing that their beliefs, ideas, values and practices are wrong or strange.

In his 1906 book, *Folkways*, sociologist William G. Sumner describes ethnocentrism as 'the technical name for the view of things in which one's own group is the centre of everything, and all others are scaled and rated with reference to it'. He further characterised ethnocentrism as often leading to pride, vanity, the belief in one's own group's superiority and contempt for outsiders.

Ethnocentrism happens largely because people have the greatest understanding of their own culture, which leads them to believe that the norms and standards of their own culture are universally adopted. A popular example of ethnocentrism is to think of the utensils different cultures prefer to use. Some cultures prefer to use knives, forks and spoons to eat, and may have the belief that it is weird or incorrect that some cultures traditionally use chopsticks or their hands.

The act of ethnocentrism is also related to racism, stereotyping, discrimination and xenophobia. This is evident when a group of individuals perceive another culture as wrong or immoral and because of this may try to convert, sometimes forcibly, the group to their own ways of living.

Other examples of ethnocentrism include:

- Judging other countries' diets and dishes;
- Expecting people to speak English if you only speak English;
- Thinking you don't have an accent and that everyone else does;
- Judging people's cultural outfits;
- Colonial imperialism;
- Delegitimising others' religious celebrations.

The first step to developing a more balanced understanding is to recognise what we don't understand. So, how can we consciously become aware of something that is happening sub-consciously? How can we know when we are being ethnocentric? Here are some starting points:

1. Watch for another's reaction – it'll tell us if our assumptions about them are incorrect. We'll see it and sense it.
2. Watch our own reactions – are we feeling uncomfortable? Are we making unfair judgements? Be introspective.
3. Control our biases – be aware of them as they arise.
4. Accept we are the learners – others know their life experiences, we do not.

F

Fundamental Attribution Error

A cognitive bias. The tendency to attribute actions by another to their character or personality while not looking for the situational explanation.

We make fundamental attribution errors (FAE) when we don't look for the reason or the situation as to why someone is behaving in a particular way. We observe someone and form an opinion about their character based on our interpretation of their actions. For example, when you meet someone for the first time, they may not appear interested in what you have to say. From your perspective it could be that they have a limited attention span, that they have more important things to do or that you are boring them. Whatever your interpretation, you will have formed an opinion about them and their character. In the workplace, for instance, there might be someone in the team who arrives late to meetings. You might then make the general assumption that they are disorganised, despite the fact that they may have only arrived late once.

Here are some starting points on how to be more mindful of how FAE might be influencing your opinions of others:

1. When you next form an opinion about someone based on their appearance, ask yourself 'Why am I doing this?' 'What am I basing my assumptions on?'
2. In a group situation, perhaps at work, what do you do when you hear others say something about someone that is an assumption? Do you seek clarity by questioning their view?
3. Think about a time when you were watching a TV show. Have you attributed the behaviour of an actor to their personality, rather than to the script?

G

Global Majority

A collective term that refers to people who are Black and indigenous and people of colour who represent over 80 per cent of the world's population. It is replacing such terms as ethnic minority.

The term global majority was first used in the early 2000s by academics. They argued that those deemed ethnic minority were in sheer numbers greater than those who were not deemed ethnic minority, and they needed a term that would reflect that. Today the term global majority can be seen in government policies, on websites, in reports on racism, in job role descriptions, in data reporting from businesses and in the curriculum of schools, further and higher education institutions.

While the discussion is evolving, the renaming to 'global majority' has helped to change people's perspective. There is recognition from various debates that, while there are more people who are part of the global majority, it does not mean that they have greater access to power. This still rests with the global minority.

Groupthink

The tendency for us to agree with each other when in a group in order to fit in and avoid conflict.

The thing about groupthink is that it happens everywhere and at any time: in families, with friends, at work, at a social meeting such as a book club. Someone might say something that we don't agree with but, as the rest of the group seems to agree, we stay silent or adopt the behaviour of others. Throughout history there have been many cases of major catastrophes where people have observed and known that the decision taken wasn't right, but they were afraid to speak up. Take a look at any newspaper where there is a scandal about a decision that a company made despite the fact that, it now comes out in hindsight, there were plenty of people who knew at the time it was a bad idea. Online groupthink is particularly tricky. We see a meme or a post that we don't like, but we might believe that if we join the debate there could be huge backlash and, quite honestly, we might not want the grief. Doing nothing even when we disagree is a by-product of groupthink.

We've all been in meetings where the leader or the most senior person expresses their view first, and immediately others in the meeting do a quick computation in their head. Do they say what they really think even if it is different from the leader's view, and risk annoying the more senior person by contradicting them in front of everyone else? What the leader should have done is wait to hear from others before expressing their view. Groupthink is costly, it can damage reputations and can be avoided. But how?

1. Make a decision that when you next disagree with a point of view, talk to a friend to test out your alternative perspective and then decide how to make your point.

2. If you get anxious at work about having to give an opinion quickly on a topic that you feel needs more thought, try saying something like 'I need a little more time on this. I'll email my views in an hour's time'.

3. As a leader of a team, encourage someone to give a contrary view even though they may not hold the view themself. Being a 'devil's advocate' can often lead to better discussion and decision-making.

H

Halo Code

First Afro hair code, a campaign pledge that guarantees Black people in the UK the freedom and security to wear their hair without restriction, judgement or discrimination.

The United States CROWN Act (Creating a Respectful and Open World for Natural hair) of 2019 is a law that prohibits race-based hair discrimination, which is the denial of opportunities because of hair texture or protective hairstyles including braids, locs, twists or bantu knots. In the UK the Halo Code was introduced in 2020 by a UK based group of activists known as the Halo Collective. The Halo Code has been adopted by major UK companies such as law firms and beauty brands.

You probably already know that when meeting someone for the first time it only takes a few seconds to assess them and a noticeable feature of the assessment is how the person looks. Hair is part of that appearance. While hair means something different to each of us, being Black with afro-textured hair has a uniquely meaningful history. (See Afro Hairstyle on page 16.)

If you are in an organisation, find out if it has adopted the Halo Code. If not, speak to your staff network group and encourage them to explore the opportunity. Better still, lead the internal discussion to create the change.

I

Implicit Bias

Bias that results from the tendency to process informa-
tion based on unconscious associations and feelings, even
when these are contrary to one's own conscious or declared
beliefs. (See Unconscious Bias on page 128.)

Inclusion

The action of including or state of being included within a
group or structure without having the need to conform.

In most organisations, the word inclusion is usually positioned next to diversity. We can see the abbreviated form of
D&I (Diversity and Inclusion) in people's job titles, on websites and policies and in reports. In the past fifteen years
or so, inclusion has become more prominent. While it is
accepted that people are diverse or different in many ways,
the challenge is how an organisation or group enables all of
its people to feel included. This same notion of inclusion is
just as important in daily life, in our families, our circle of
friends as well as work colleagues. This is because inclusion is
now closely aligned to belonging (see page 28), as belonging
is what people feel as a result of inclusive behaviours, such
as using inclusive language, keeping up to date on inclusion
topics, sharing knowledge with colleagues and calling out
non-inclusive behaviours.

Try to recall a time when someone made you feel really
included in a discussion. They may have agreed or not with

your view but they probably thanked you and encouraged you to say more. Ask yourself:

1. Have you experienced the benefits of inclusion? If you were invited to write a blog about the topic, what would be your top three points?
2. Imagine that a friend was asked about your inclusive behaviours. What would they say?
3. Think of someone you like professionally because they demonstrate inclusive behaviours. What are three things that you like about them, and three examples of things they have done to make you feel included?

Inclusive Language

Language that avoids expressions that are considered to express or imply ideas that are harmful to any particular group of people.

The intention of inclusive language is to encourage us to think about the language we use. Being conscious of what we say and write is important. We don't want to cause offence; we want to demonstrate that we are thoughtful and, above all, we want to know how to avoid making embarrassing remarks.

Inclusive language shares the characteristics of other languages. There is a grammar and a vocabulary and it is capable of change. And, as with other languages, how and why the language changes and who instigates the change can be difficult to pinpoint. The current use of pronouns is an example of gender language changing. Increasingly, individuals are deciding how they wish to be addressed. For some she/her or he/him is no longer appropriate and they may prefer they/them or other combinations. Some may say siblings rather than brother or sister.

There is also much debate about the ownership of language and the use of the 'right' terminology. For example, who has the authority to say some words and not others and who makes that call? If you belong to a particular religious group, is it okay for you to say things about your own religion that, if said by someone not of your faith, would be deemed offensive? When it comes to race, that is where people often get into difficulty with inclusive language. There is a complex web of historical injustice represented through words and understanding this takes conscious effort. If you are unsure about a specific word and whether or not it is inclusive, we hope that this book is a useful resource.

Indirect Discrimination

A practice, policy or rule that applies to everyone in the same way but has a detrimental effect on some people more than others.

Sometimes discrimination can be easy to spot. It's blatant and you can't miss it – for example, if a hotel turns you away because of your sexuality. This is called direct discrimination. But there are other times when a policy has a detrimental effect on someone because of who they are. For example, someone who wears a symbol of faith and is placed on leave at work as the company policy states that no jewellery can be visible. Another example would be a company policy that requires employees to have 'professional' hairstyles, which could indirectly discriminate against Black people who might wear their hair in natural styles such as locs, Afros, braids or twists. This is also discrimination and the UK Equality Act 2010 calls this indirect discrimination.

We don't want to get into a legal discussion here, but it's worth noting that you can only challenge a practice, policy or rule which you think is indirectly discriminatory if it affects you personally. This means that you have to raise the issue, seek advice and see the complaint process through.

Inequality

An unfair situation in society where some people have more opportunities than others.

Inequality is not a new phenomenon. While the legal frameworks that govern society have developed, such as new or amended legislation, the principle of inequality continues to evoke a discussion about morals. No matter the historical period, inequality is always in opposition to equality and the discussion is usually around the dynamics of status (social disparity), rights (justice) and opportunities (distribution of resources). There are many reports by charities, think tanks and academic institutions that examine the relationship between inequality and race. For instance, research by The Equality & Human Rights Commission found that Black workers with degrees earn 23.1 per cent less on average than White workers, and that Black people who leave school with A-levels typically get paid 14.3 per cent less than their White peers. In education, Black Caribbean and Mixed White/Black Caribbean children have rates of permanent exclusion about three times that of the pupil population as a whole.

In a way, inequality can be the basis of effective storytelling. Someone has hardship and then makes good. We particularly like the film *Hidden Figures*, a true story about some amazing African American female mathematicians who contributed significantly to the work at NASA in the 1960s. Take a look and share with your friends the scenes that particularly shocked and inspired you.

Intersectionality

The interconnected nature of social categorisations, such as race, class and gender as they apply to a given individual or group. It is regarded as creating overlapping and interdependent systems of discrimination or disadvantage.

The concept of intersectionality was introduced to the field of legal studies by Black feminist scholar Kimberlé Crenshaw, who used the term in two essays published in 1989 and 1991. While the theory primarily began as an exploration of the oppression of Black women within society and the ways in which they experience intersecting layers of different forms of oppression, the analysis has expanded to include many more aspects of social identity.

The nine protected characteristics enshrined in UK law (age, disability, gender reassignment, marriage and civil partnership, pregnancy and maternity, race, religion or belief, sex, and sexual orientation) are the elements that interlink with each other. There are other areas that could be and often are included in conversations of intersectionality, such as class.

Intersectionality shows how different elements of identity link to shape our unique experiences. We use intersectionality to show the disadvantages caused by intersecting systems against others in society. Take the example of a Black person with a disability. They will probably experience racism as well as ableism. Another example is of a Black person who identifies as LGBTQIA+. They will most likely have challenges related to both homophobia and racism. There are arguments about intersectionality being a more important focus than discussions on any single element, such as race. We would argue that it's not either/or, and that learning more about racial discourse is a way to also understand intersectionality, and vice versa.

Think of how you would describe your intersectional self. Use the nine protected characteristics above and reflect on which characteristic you would start with and why. Give yourself one point if you have experienced discrimination in any one of the characteristics. For example, score a point if you have experienced discrimination because of your sex, race, age, disability, religion and so on. Total your points. Ask a couple of friends to do the same and have a conversation about your scores and the examples of discrimination experienced.

J

Jazzieness

Someone who improvises their use of language, demonstrating the ability to adapt to different cultures.

Many of you might think of jazz when you see jazzieness. As a musical expression, jazz contains improvisation and takes inspiration from different cultural styles and genres. In our definition we look at the use of language in a similar way. Today if you hear someone being described as having jazzieness it means that they consciously play with their use of language in different cultural contexts. They appear to be a confident communicator, are able to think on their feet and enjoy doing so.

However, this is not about mimicking someone's accent or adopting phrases or sayings. Jazzieness embraces respect, humbleness and authenticity. We can learn the difference by reading the many poets who are jazzie. We like Grace Nichols' work that is currently studied by GCSE English Literature students in the UK. Her poetry often explores themes of identity and she uses vivid imagery, powerful metaphors and a strong sense of cultural identity to explore complex themes and issues. When you read her poems out loud they have a syncopation about them.

Jazzie Activity

With a friend choose a topic (such as the weather) and improvise around it. Start with an incomplete statement that your friend will finish. For example, 'the clouds . . .' '. . . are high in the sky'. 'Today the rain . . .' '. . . was thunderous and I got soaked'.

When you have finished laughing, tell a story together using the same technique, but this time talk about your differences and similarities.

K

Knee (Taking the)

The action of getting down on one knee as a symbolic gesture against racism.

Taking the knee is a political performance of protest. It originated in the 1780s by British abolitionists who designed a cameo modelled by Josiah Wedgwood, William Weber and William Hackwood. The cameo depicted a Black enslaved man on his knee asking the question 'Am I not a man and a brother?' This image of supplication and prayer was an attempt to focus public attention to the evils of enslavement. The posture then manifested during the American civil rights movement through an image of Martin Luther King Jr kneeling in 1965 to protest against the lack of voting rights for African American people.

Taking the knee took on a new trajectory in 2016 when American football sportsmen Colin Kaepernick, Eli Harold and Eric Reid knelt on one knee during the American national anthem in a response to Black men being killed by police in the United States. It grew again in prominence during 2020 as a result of the murder by police of George Floyd and has since taken on global significance as a silent gesture of solidarity, often performed at the start of sporting events as a reminder of racial injustice.

L

Language of Race (Black)

The system of words, behaviour and signs that people use to express thoughts, emotions and feelings relating to the experience of being Black.

We wrote this book to help people keep up to date with the language of race from the perspective of being Black. Language evolves and being intentional about the words we use shows respect for individuals and communities. For example, using terms that Black people prefer to use to describe themselves rather than relying on words and phrases you might have used while growing up that are now outdated.

Being contemporary in our use of language enables better communication with people different from ourselves. If we are intentional and alert about our use of language, we can avoid perpetuating assumptions and stereotypes. We can acknowledge people's differences positively.

Lived Experience

Personal knowledge about the world gained through direct first-hand engagement in everyday events rather than through representations constructed by other people.

The term 'lived experience' is mainly used in phenomenology research – a form of qualitative research that investigates people's everyday lives – where the researchers suspend preconceived assumptions, but people have increasingly started to use it outside of a research context. More and more of us are using the term as we legitimise ourselves and our views, to shift the focus away from being talked about and towards first-hand personal experience. The impact of lived experience becomes lived reality. Lived experience is to do with an individual's interpretation of events and can vary extensively from person to person, even in similar situations. Each person's experience is valid and valuable, providing insights and knowledge that may not be apparent to others.

On the other hand, lived reality takes into account social, political, economic and cultural factors that influence a person's life and affect their opportunities and overall future.

When we have the opportunity to share our lived experiences, it can be uplifting and reaffirming. It's also a way of informing and educating those around us to be unafraid to ask questions and be curious without fear of recrimination. When we hear stories, how well do we listen? Listening involves paying attention, asking questions and having the desire to understand.

Lupinesque

To use one's Blackness for good.

In 1907 author Maurice Leblanc wrote about a fictional French gentleman thief Arsène Lupin. Lupin was a master of disguise and often operated on the wrong side of the law, despite being a force for good. As a marketing stunt, Omar Sy – who played a character inspired by Lupin in the 2021 Netflix TV series of the same name – spent a day with a bucket and brush gluing up his own billboard posters on the Paris metro. At 6ft 2in tall and dressed in overalls, he wondered if people would recognise him. What he found was that appearing as a low-paid maintenance person made him invisible and that people made negative judgements about him.

Lupinesque is a word used in communities of Black people. It is used as a shorthand to mean that someone is able to intentionally disguise themself for the good of others or that they have deliberately chosen to disguise something about themself which they plan to reveal later. It is unlikely that they can make the colour of their skin invisible, but they use their Blackness to be a role model for others. For example, the accomplished footballer Marcus Rashford and his campaign on free school meals did not lead with the colour of his skin but focused on child food poverty. Another example is Stormzy, who launched the Stormzy Scholarship for Black UK students in 2018 at the University of Cambridge. He created a pathway for Black students to succeed in their studies and removed barriers by using his economic power for good. Both these individuals ventured into areas outside of their profession and positively influenced the lives of others.

M

Microaffirmations

Small and often subtle actions of inclusion that give the receiver a feeling of being valued and a sense of belonging.

Saying 'thank you', making eye contact, acknowledging an accomplishment are all examples of microaffirmations and they make others feel valued. They build trust, foster positive relationships and contribute to a more inclusive and supportive culture, particularly in professional contexts. Think about a time when you were in a meeting and someone whose opinion you valued nodded in agreement with a point that you were making. It would have boosted your confidence and made you feel good.

A person who consciously uses microaffirmations has a mature understanding of diversity, equity and inclusion. They know that a smile, a nod of recognition does not take much effort and that these subtle acts of appreciation signal acceptance and respect for others.

Try being intentional about microaffirmations. You could recognise someone in a team meeting for the work that they have done. You might have seen someone staying late at work to support another colleague to meet a deadline, and a microaffirmation would be sending an email to the two colleagues to express your appreciation of their team work.

Microaggressions

Everyday slights, put-downs and insults in the form of statements, actions or incidents that are indirect, subtle or unintentional against members of a marginalised group.

Psychiatrist Chester Pierce is attributed with coining the term microaggression during the 1960s. Pierce defined microaggressions as Black–White interactions characterised by White put-downs, done in an automatic, preconscious or unconscious fashion. In 2010 Derald Wing Sue expanded on Pierce's observations by suggesting that microaggressions are becoming more invisible, subtle and indirect, operating below the level of conscious awareness, and continue to oppress in unseen ways.

The difficulty with microaggressions is that they can be blatant and obvious as well as being invisible and subtle. This makes knowing and describing when a microaggression has occurred more challenging to pinpoint. Asking a Black person 'Where are you from, no really from?' or telling them that they are articulate are examples of microaggressions. For example, asking someone where they are from may appear fairly innocuous, but implicitly delivers a message that the person being asked the question is an outsider. When someone says 'You are articulate', this appears to compliment a person's intelligence but actually it reinforces negative stereotypes that it is remarkable for a Black person to be articulate, and is insulting.

When a person first experiences a microaggression it comes as a shock. No matter how many times they experience a microaggression, it continues to be a shock. Psychologists describe microaggressions as death by a thousand cuts. Over time microaggressions create inner conflict and chronic stress. They chip away at an individual's self-worth, negatively affecting their mental, emotional and physical health.

We all have a responsibility to be conscious of how our words and behaviours affect another person. Taking the time to understand the different forms of microaggressions is a step towards this. If you are a witness to a microaggression don't stand by: speak up. You could ask for clarification along the lines of 'Please say more about what you mean by that' or you could say, 'That's a stereotype. I've learned that . . .'

What about a colleague who tells you about their experience of a recent microaggression during a team meeting? Perhaps they described how another team member told a joke that was offensive and, when concerns were raised, they were told not to be so sensitive. As you listen to your colleague, empathise with them by saying 'I can see why you would take offence and be angry about this situation. Why not have a quiet chat with a few other team members to get their support just in case this happens again?' Others may step in before you do and if they do, thank them.

There are three other words associated with microaggressions:

microassault, **microinsult** and **microinvalidation**.

An example of each is:

- **Microassault:** Microassaults are overt actions and involve explicit expressions of intentional discrimination. They are small actions (whether spoken or through behaviour) and include racial slurs or doing something to another without their permission. For example, touching a Black person's hair.
- **Microinsult:** A microinsult is a comment, action or gesture that conveys a negative message. It appears harmless and innocent but it contains underlying biases and prejudices. For example, telling a Black person that they are 'articulate'.
- **Microinvalidation**: This type of microaggression involves dismissing or minimising the experience or feelings of another based on their identity. It can take many forms but often involves subtle messaging that experiences

are not valid or important. For example, when someone says to a Black person that they don't see colour.

Misogynoir

A type of discrimination towards Black women where both race and gender play a role in bias.

In order to understand misogynoir it's helpful to look at 'misogyny', which is a term meaning a hatred of women. The term 'misogynoir' was coined by Black feminist Moya Bailey in 2010, combining misogyny and the French word 'noir', meaning Black.

When hate is directed to a Black woman, this is misogynoir. It specifically refers to the intersection of racism and sexism and can take many forms including negative stereotypes and microaggressions. For example, when Black women speak out on injustices, they often receive online abuse and harassment. Misogynoir is evident in everyday life and you might have seen it operating. Look at Meghan Markle, Duchess of Sussex. The vitriol directed at her is unrelenting and there's a real hatred in the comments made in the media.

When misogynists vent about Black women, what they are really displaying is insecurity and fear; to see a Black woman who has dared to speak up and raise her head regardless of the consequences upsets their view of what the world order should be.

Be intentional about understanding misogynoir. You can develop your knowledge by talking to a friend to see if they have any views on this. Extend the discussion by exploring what you might do if you saw or experienced misogynoir. Take a look at the many resources online and share the information with a work colleague.

Multiculturalism

The presence of, or support for the presence of, several distinct cultural or ethnic groups.

Multicultural ideals have existed since ancient times. Throughout history we can see how various nations have welcomed different people into their national identity. One example is the Roman Empire (27 BC–476 AD) that was known for its policy of granting citizenship to non-Roman people. The Romans encouraged the creation of voluntary associations, professional and trade guilds, religious groups and arts societies in order to welcome those from a different cultural heritage. Another example is the Islamic Golden Age (eighth to the fourteenth centuries); a time when Islamic culture flourished and Muslim scholars made significant contributions to astronomy, mathematics and philosophy. The period was marked by a tolerance of multiculturalism and a spirit of intellectual inquiry.

Often multiculturalism is associated with migrants and immigration policies. The term is political, hotly debated and raises fundamental issues about national identity and how host nations adjust to the customs and values of different people. Today multiculturalism is seen as an outdated phrase when linked to immigration, governments and policies. We are more likely to hear about social cohesion and diversity.

N

Name Bias

Making negative judgements of people based on their name(s).

Name bias is the tendency to discriminate against people based solely on their name. Judgements about culture and race are made in response to a name, normally one that is not Anglo sounding, and they create an automatic disadvantage and exclusion.

It is particularly prevalent in job applications, where candidates with the skills and qualifications for a role are sometimes not called for interviews because assumptions are made based on their name sounding African or Black. As a consequence, many organisations (universities, UK civil service, private sector companies, non-profits and so on) have started to remove candidate names from applications in order to create a more dynamic and diverse workforce and limit unconscious bias from the sifting process. Name redaction has led to fairer representation at interview stage and better hiring outcomes.

Names create a sense of belonging, unity and familial recognition. They are part of our personal brand. Many names have meanings that connect to heritage and ancestral lineage. When our name is used incorrectly it can trigger feelings of rejection or dismissal of that heritage. Today more people are including phonetic pronunciation and the spelling of their names in their email signature, so there is no reason to say or write people's names incorrectly. It takes a little intentional effort.

When we address people by pronouncing their name correctly, it shows respect. We might get the pronunciation wrong in the first instance but it shouldn't happen again. Ask someone how their name is pronounced. Then repeat the name to check that you have heard correctly and write the name down phonetically.

Non-Racist

Someone who does nothing to positively change the negative race situation in society.

A non-racist person is different from an anti-racist (see page 21) person. A non-racist will not necessarily hold racist beliefs or engage in racist behaviour but they will benefit from and perpetuate racist systems and structures, often unknowingly. They will not actively work to challenge or change these systems.

An anti-racist is someone who recognises that racism is a systemic problem and that it affects individuals and communities in many ways. They work to dismantle the systems and structures that perpetuate racial inequality through, for example: education such as this book; advocacy by speaking or writing about racism; and supporting initiatives that aim to promote equity for all people.

How would you describe yourself – non-racist or anti-racist? How might your friends or co-workers describe you?

O

Oppression

An unjust exercise of power or authority at an individual or systematic level.

Oppression is observed and experienced and comes in many forms. It is what people do to others and includes exploitation, violence and marginalisation. It is also systemic and woven into the fabric of society. We can think of oppression by looking at '-isms'; those attitudes, actions or institutional structures that oppress a person or group because of their connection to a marginalised group, such as disability (ableism), economic status (classism), sexual orientation (heterosexism), older age (ageism), race (racism), religion (e.g. anti-Islam), language/immigrant status (xenophobism), country (ethnocentrism), gender (sexism).

In order to identify oppression, you will need to be curious about why it affects some people. Think of those who are denied access to employment opportunities because of the colour of their skin. This practice is oppressive and illegal. What about when someone is denied access to good housing because of their economic status and race? This is oppression.

We recommend three things that you can do to help your understanding of and to combat oppression:

1. Examine your own privilege and consider how you may be contributing to oppressive policies and practices.
2. Research the charity sector and get involved with one that serves disadvantaged communities.
3. In your professional life, look out for policies that may unintentionally disadvantage and be oppressive to certain groups; for example, those with a strong religious Black church affiliation.

P

Person of Colour (POC)

Someone who is not White.

Person or people of colour (POC) has an interesting history. We see references to people of colour in citations written in the eighteenth century in relation to slavery and also of how it was used interchangeably with the word 'coloured'. Today, POC is no longer used interchangeably with 'coloured'. Coloured has been viewed as a pejorative word, while some parts of the world such as South Africa use coloured as a term for a racial group. There are also a number of United States associations that have coloured in their title e.g. National Association for the Advancement of Colored People formed in 1909 or the National Association of Colored Women's Clubs formed in 1904. In the UK there have been a few associations that had coloured in their title but they no longer exist; we are more likely to view coloured as offensive.

While POC is primarily used in the United States, it has been adopted by others in mainly English-speaking nations such as the UK, Canada, Australia and Ireland. Interestingly, sometimes POC is used by people who find it difficult to say Black. How do you feel about using the term?

Positive Action

Taking specific steps to improve equality and equity.

Positive action, affirmative action and positive discrimination are often confused with each other. What each of them has in common is that they are used in the context of employment and the workplace. In the UK, two are legal and one illegal. Let's deal with the legal phrases.

In the UK Equality Act 2010 positive action allows the selection of a candidate from an 'under-represented' group, so long as they are no less than equally qualified compared to another potential candidate who is not from the under-represented group. Affirmative action (see page 12) is from the United States and came into practice in 1961. It works in the same way as positive action. Positive discrimination is illegal; we look at this on page 109.

While positive action is voluntary, many organisations have developed robust reasoning around their positive action policies. Rather than favouring an individual because they have a protected characteristic (which is a criticism often levied against positive action), it manifests in actions like talent initiatives. Reflect on what you think about positive action. Do you think it is right that under-represented people benefit from positive action in the workplace? Why?

Here are some examples of positive action initiatives that organisations can implement:

1. Refresh diversity, equity and inclusion training programmes so that topics remain current.
2. Provide mentoring, sponsorship and coaching opportunities so that people can be successful in their roles with the right support.
3. Undertake outreach and recruitment activities by partnering with community organisations, attending job fairs and advertising in publications that target specific groups.
4. Promote flexible working arrangements, such as remote working or flexible hours, to accommodate the needs of

employees who face barriers to full participation in the workplace.

5. Develop bias-free recruitment and selection processes. Eliminate bias by using structured, competency-based interview techniques, hidden CV screening and software that detects bias in job adverts and interview questions.

Positive Discrimination

When preferential treatment is given to people with a protected characteristic.

Positive discrimination is sometimes confused with positive action, but it is significant to note that positive discrimination is unlawful. There are exceptions to this, but they only apply to very specific situations where employers can show that there is a genuine occupational requirement (for example, someone's sex to provide personal care).

Automatic favouring without proper consideration of merit of under-represented individuals from minority groups over individuals in majority groups is discriminatory. For example, it would be unlawful to set a quota to recruit or promote a specific proportion of people from a protected characteristic group. If you are involved with recruitment – and it could be for a voluntary role – recall the training you received to ensure that there was an understanding about discrimination.

Here are some examples of positive discrimination that are illegal:

1. A policy or practice that prioritises women over men for a job that does not require gender specific skills or qualifications;

2. A practice of reverse discrimination when members of a majority group are discriminated against in favour of members of a minority group;
3. When employers set aside promotions for specific groups of under-represented people that are not based on merit.

Q

Quota

Having a number/percentage stated to correct an imbalance of under-represented groups.

The use of quotas in relation to equality has always been controversial. The UK Equalities Act 2010 prohibits the use of quotas to achieve greater representation of certain groups. While there is no consensus on the merits of quotas, more organisations are now able to articulate their views on why they do not use them, going beyond the legal framework and discussing the moral position.

While quotas may not be allowed, thinking about proportionality from an inclusion perspective is. Most businesses will say something like: last year we recruited 49 per cent male and 51 per cent female graduates, and we expect that progression will be proportionate. But if, three years down the line, only 30 per cent of associates are female, this would require a deeper dive. Why are proportionally more men being promoted than women? The other issue is that quotas are sometimes used interchangeably with targets. Targets are aspirational. The *Parker Review* reported on the lack of ethnic diversity on FTSE 100 Boards and had a mission to encourage companies to work on 'more than one before 2021'.

As a strategy it appears to be working, as more Boards have greater representation. In 2022, the *Parker Review* announced its results of its voluntary census. It stated that 96 per cent of FTSE 100 companies had met the target with at least one minority ethnic director on their boards, up from 89 per cent the previous year. Of the 96 FTSE 100 companies, 49 per cent had more than one minority ethnic director on their board.

R

Racial Literacy

Having the knowledge, skills, awareness and disposition to talk about race and racism.

We might start by saying that literacy is the ability to read, speak and write confidently. A literate person is able to express themself with fluency and understands how meaning can be interpreted to make sense of the world. We apply this axiom to racial literacy. Just as you would expect most children to be able to read, write and speak with growing confidence, we should also expect adults to have an awareness of racial literacy. This book is a good starting point.

We believe that being literate is not just about reading, speaking and writing or having knowledge of a particular academic subject. It's to do with being literate about life.

A Black parent will have ensured that their children have read books, played with toys, listened to music that represents them positively. They will have taught them that racism exists in many guises. If you are not a Black parent, you will have ensured that your children have read books that represent diversity in a positive and educational way. It may be that you have teenage children who are teaching you.

Take a moment to ask yourself the following:

1. If someone visited your home and looked at your books, would they say that you have racial literacy? If not a book, what could you point out to them to show your racial literacy?
2. At work, are you aware of any discussion on racial literacy? If not, how could you introduce it? If yes, what did you find out?

Racism

Racism in its many forms is everywhere and anyone who knows what to look for can see and feel it. While racism can be applied to different communities within society, we explore it through the specific lens of racism against Black people.

If you are in a social setting and hear a friend telling a racist joke or comment, speak up. Do so in your way, but make sure your point has been understood. You may lose a friend but you will gain many more, and you may have helped your friend appreciate how jokes can cause offence. At work, if you are leading a team, have an inclusion moment once a month at the start of a regular meeting. You could begin by talking about what you understand by one of the following types of racism and develop the discussion to relate it to your team's work:

Anti-
The policy or practice of actively opposing racism and promoting racial tolerance. (See page 21.)

Commoditised
Using colour of skin overtly as an advantage to market and sell.

There are a number of examples in advertising where messages have been ill-judged and not very clever. Think of sports, beauty and fashion brands; some have tried to benefit from associating their product with Black identity. For example, a drinks company advert featured a celebrity giving a police officer a drink during a Black Lives Matter protest. Many people, particularly on social media, posted that the advert was insensitive and offensive. Another example was a clothing brand that had in their advert a caricature of a Black person with language that was deemed racist and perpetuated negative stereotypes. In both of these instances, the companies commoditised their product. Usually, this leads to the company rescinding the advertisement.

Covert

The subtle but intentional and harmful attitudes or behaviours towards another person because of the colour of their skin, often disguised by evasive or passive methods.

Covert racism is subtle, unspoken and private. It is to do with cognitive processes, a person's internal dialogue and thoughts, and it can't be observed. While we can't get inside someone's head, we can see behaviours such as facial expressions or body language and gestures that show intentional and negative attitudes towards others. For example, a Black female barrister arrived at court and was mistaken as the defendant. The security officer asked what her name was so that he could find it on the list of defendants. Covert racism can only be observed once the thought translates into an action.

Institutional

The collective failure of an organisation to provide an appropriate service to people because of their colour, culture or ethnic origin.

Organisations tend to have limited understanding of how institutional racism works. An organisation is made up of people and people are its culture. If an organisation has institutional racism in it, it follows that it is because some people within behave in ways that are unlawful, discriminatory and racist.

Some ways to see institutional racism include:

1. Historical context. What is the history of the organisation?
2. Systemic patterns. Are there policies, practices and procedures that disadvantage Black people?
3. Disparate outcomes. Are Black people consistently experiencing negative outcomes compared to others, such as not being selected to work on a project?
4. Power structures. Is the decision-making concentrated in the hands of a particular racial group and does this group consistently make decisions that disadvantage other groups?

Overt

The intentional and/or obvious harmful attitudes or behaviours towards another person because of the colour of their skin.

Overt racism is when racist thoughts turn into behaviour that is observable. For example, imagine there is a networking opportunity at work and for some reason it has excluded Black people. How could this have happened given that there are some Black people in the organisation? Perhaps it is that the majority of Black people are lower down the organisational tree, and the person in charge of the guest list decided junior team members would not be invited. To our minds, this is covert racism that became overt.

Structural
Laws, rules or official policies in a society that result in and support a continued unfair advantage to some people and unfair or harmful treatment of others based on the colour of their skin.

Structural racism can be thought of as a framework on which other things are assembled. Think of it as the building you live in, with its walls, ceilings and windows. We assemble the contents in and around our house to make it comfortable and we call it our home. If there is racism in those foundational structures of an organisation – its rules, culture and acceptable behaviour – then it doesn't matter how great the interior design is, it will remain a racist place. It could be that you are learning a European language and note that none of the examples in the teaching materials mention or even show images of Black people. This is a structural issue; the content has been developed over decades and is unlikely to change, even with student contributions.

Systemic
Policies and practices that exist throughout a whole society or organisation, and that result in and support a continued unfair advantage to some people and unfair or harmful treatment of others based on the colour of their skin.

Systemic racism refers to the ways in which racism is embedded in everyday life. It can be found in policies, practices and procedures of organisations. For example, the disproportionate representation of Black people in the criminal justice system who are more likely to be arrested, convicted and sentenced to longer prison terms compared to White individuals for the same crimes.

Other disparities that highlight systemic racism can be found in the healthcare system. Black people often experience unequal access to health, including access to insurance, preventative care and treatment for chronic diseases. Another example is in employment. The systemic barriers include discrimination in hiring, pay inequality and lack of Black people in leadership positions.

Think about how you feel after reading about the various forms of racism outlined above. Reflect on the words that give you an 'a-ha' moment and why this might be the case. Consider your own examples of each kind of racism and how you would spot it at work, at home, in a social setting and in society.

S

Stereotype Bias

An unfair view that people have about Black people based on oversimplified and untrue ideas or images.

The etymology of stereotype comes from the Greek word 'stereos' meaning solid and 'typos' meaning impression. Stereotype bias is informed by various sources such as the media, cultural norms, personal experiences and societal structures. These biases can affect our perceptions, attitudes and behaviours towards others, often resulting in unfair treatment and discrimination.

People are often biased against others outside of their own social group, showing prejudice (emotional bias), stereotypes (cognitive bias) and discrimination (behavioural bias). From a race perspective, stereotype bias has been around for centuries. Look at any historical text of the nineteenth century and there will be images, commentary and views that summarise a group of people negatively based on their characteristics. Queen Victoria was on the throne, slavery was abolished in Europe and the Americas, and Britain was a major colonial power. Black people were stereotyped as being lazy and not very intelligent, for example.

One way that stereotype bias works is that we believe things by omission. If there are no Black people in Western European classical orchestras, we might therefore wrongly assume that Black people do not like classical music. Or that Black people are brilliant at athletics but not good at swimming because we haven't seen them in major sports fixtures or in the local community swimming pools. But not only is this reductive as it only looks at a small sample size, it also doesn't consider the complex set of historical, political, societal and economic factors that stop people doing things.

Here are five ways to spot stereotype bias in yourself:

1. Ask yourself if you make assumptions about others based on their race or other characteristics.
2. Are your beliefs about different groups of people based on your personal experiences?
3. Do you consciously broaden your understanding of different groups of people by, for example, having conversations with people from different backgrounds?
4. When you hear someone making a stereotype joke, do you speak up and challenge it?
5. Are you open to receiving feedback if someone points out that you have exhibited stereotype bias?

T

Third Culture Individual

Someone who has a blended cultural identity that is different from that of their parents or of their country of nationality.

Due to globalisation there are growing numbers of people who identify as a third culture individual. They will have spent some of their childhood living outside of their parents' country or that of their nationality and will have experience navigating between different cultural expectations and norms. This experience often results in the individual developing a hybrid identity that is different from their parents' culture. As a result, they may have a heightened cultural awareness, empathy and an ability to communicate across cultural boundaries.

Tokenism

The practice of making a symbolic effort to seem inclusive to members of minority groups without meaningful structural change.

From our point of view, tokenism is not a good thing. It is often associated with employment and is about the representation of a numerical minority in an organisation. Tokenism is often described as a solution, earnest in effort but, in reality, it only acknowledges an issue without actually solving it. For example, a start-up company may think that having a Black person in their publicity campaign will attract more customers. Another example is when an international global awards ceremony has a host who is Black but there are no Black nominees for awards.

Many organisations strive to have greater diversity in their workforce and know that visible diversity is important to internal and external relations. An organisation may want to see greater ethnic minority representation at certain levels of seniority or clients may push hard for diversity in project teams. While this is all good, it is the way of achieving diversity that can give rise to tokenism. Too often we hear that someone believes or has been told that the reason they got a job was because they are Black. If the statement is true, then this would be an example of poor recruitment decision making. If untrue, there will be work to do so that everyone understands that the decision was made on capabilities and not identity.

Tokenism is lonely, and being the only one or one of a few people who share identities can feel isolating. People who have become tokens might not have colleagues to turn to for support. They may be extremely visible in an organisation and yet also invisible. Being visible can come with scrutiny and pressure to represent an entire group, often adding huge amounts of extra workload and emotional labour (see page 66). People who are tokens often experience anxiety and stress and might even be tempted to overwork in order to try to be a 'good' representative of that identity group. In addition, their professional achievements may go unacknowledged or their contributions ignored.

At work, listen to discussions on how a team plans to increase its client or customer base. If you hear someone say something along the lines of, 'Let's have a woman, a Black man and a person with a disability on our website', be the one to question whether the idea could be viewed as tokenism.

Tone Policing

Attacking the tone in which a statement was presented rather than the message itself to detract from its validity.

When people tone police, they are more concerned with the delivery of the message rather than its content and attack the person rather than their argument. The notion of tone policing became prominent in the United States in 2010 when feminist and anti-racism advocates started calling it out.

Tone policing has a particular resonance with Black people, who are often portrayed as angry, loud and aggressive. Examples of tone policing include a Black person sharing their experience of microaggressions in the workplace and someone responding with, 'You are overreacting.' Or if a Black person talks about their fear of being stopped by the police and they are met with, 'You're just being paranoid. Not all members of the police are bad.' Or if a Black person speaks out about an unfair promotion process and they are told 'You need to be more objective and look at the facts.'

Reflect on a time when you dismissed what someone was saying because of the way they delivered their message. You might think of a politician. When talking to friends did you describe the politician and not the perspective?

U

Unconscious Bias

Prejudiced, unsupported, unconscious judgements in favour of or against one thing, person or group as compared to another, in a way that is usually considered unfair. (See Implicit Bias on page 81.)

The term implicit bias was first coined in 1995 by psychologists Mahzarin Banaji and Anthony Greenwald, where they argued that social behaviour is largely influenced by unconscious associations and judgments (Greenwald & Banaji, 1995). It is generally understood that implicit bias and unconscious bias refer to the same thing and can be used interchangeably.

People often want to know where unconscious bias comes from. They may say that they have no biases. Yet what we think and ultimately do is based on a complex web of life experiences, background and values which help us make sense of the world. It is this web that creates our biases. Even though we receive thousands of clues every day about people different from ourselves, we can still rely on stereotypes about them to form our opinions and behaviours. If you follow this logic, it is difficult to argue that someone has no biases.

Once accepted that unconscious bias exists, it follows that we want to know how to make them conscious. One thing to remember is that deprogramming your biases takes time. It involves pausing and asking yourself why you feel discomfort about someone or something. Be honest. It is through honesty that you will uncover your biases and make them conscious. Learn to slow down before jumping to conclusions. Try taking perspective – look beyond your own point of view so that you can consider how someone else may think or feel about something. Display empathy.

Here are some starting pointers:

1. Think about someone different from you and jot down why they are not in your social or professional networks. Now turn the situation around and jot down why you think you are not in their networks.
2. Have you taken the Harvard University Implicit Association Test to find out some of your biases? Why not take the test?
3. Let's do a simple three-step experiment. Look at the contacts in your phone and on a scale of one to ten (one = least; ten = most) note how many of your contacts look like you. Look again at your full list and now note how many share your social interests. Look one last time and score how many have values that align with yours. Chances are that most people are common in all three points but what of the few who you hardly know. Could you be missing opportunities here?

V

Virtue Signalling

The act of pretending to be virtuous rather than having genuine passion for an issue.

There is no credible evidence of who coined the phrase or when it was first used, but we do know it is a contemporary, triggering phrase with negative connotations. Virtue signalling is something that people call out about the actions of others – usually companies and brands. For example, a business that runs a PR campaign about its commitment to Black suppliers in response to the Black Lives Matter movement might claim that they are socially responsible. While at first glance this appears laudable, it does raise the issue of their diversity credentials and if the company is self-promoting by announcing this to the world.

Social media is a place where there is much virtue signalling. People are motivated in the virtual world to appear good as it wins them friends and social status. Individuals position themselves as doing the right thing and appear boastful of the fact that, for example, they have donated funds to a charity.

Think about where you work and whether its response to the George Floyd murder in May 2020 was effective. Reflect on why there was a positive response, no response or an inadequate one. A positive response would have been to acknowledge the tragedy and publicly express support for those who had been affected; creating a space for dialogue for colleagues to share their feelings and experiences related to racial injustice and police brutality; committing to actions that are sustainable, such as investing funds in Black businesses to help them grow.

Organisations that gave no response to the murder were seen as not caring about Black people. The message sent was that race issues were not a priority; a lack of response had a negative impact on the organisation's reputation particularly on social media. Also, there was a lack of trust from employees and customers.

Some organisations gave an inadequate response such as issuing a generic statement expressing condolences without a plan or commitment to address race issues; making token-istic gestures such as diversity training that avoided the issues of inequality.

W

White Privilege

Inherent advantages that a White person is unaware they have over a Black person, which automatically excludes or protects them from certain negative experiences.

White privilege is not a new social phenomenon and it is a phrase that can strongly divide people. For decades Black academics, authors, filmmakers and many others have commented on White privilege. Probably due to the Black Lives Matter movement gaining greater attention through social media, White privilege is often hotly debated from an emotional perspective. Some argue that privilege has nothing to do with the colour of a person's skin. We respectfully disagree.

We think of White privilege as an absence of awareness of what it is to be Black. This is not about empathy but rather the basic aspects of life that White people don't even think about. For example, if a Black person is stopped by the police at a train station, can you be sure that they haven't been singled out because of their colour?

And here is the bit that hurts. Most Black people know the privileges of being White. We see it around us all of the time. As you read about White privilege, think about how you feel deep down about it. You may have positive or negative responses that are emotionally based and that is fine; it is better to acknowledge this than not. Commit to talking about it with others.

Woke

A mindset of self-awareness of issues that concern social justice and racial equality.

In 1923, a collection of aphorisms and ideas by the Jamaican philosopher and social activist Marcus Garvey included the summons 'Wake up Ethiopia! Wake up Africa!' as a call to global Black citizens to become more socially and politically conscious. The word woke came from the phrase 'stay woke' which emerged in the 1930s in African American vernacular English and referred to a raising of awareness to the political and social issues affecting African Americans. By the mid-twentieth century woke had become a global term to mean being well informed or being aware of issues around racial injustice, especially in a political or cultural sense.

From 2008, it was used increasingly by political and social commentators in both positive and negative ways. Like many borrowed words taken out of context, woke was given a new meaning. Social media posts were full of woke pride and it was something that young adults said to their parents to educate them. It was also a word that was used in a pejorative way. The term cancel culture emerged in opposition to woke. Cancel culture is when someone is called out for saying something that is deemed offensive. The calling out usually takes place on social media and gathers huge followers demanding that the person be sacked from their job, lose their sponsorship and/or be forced to retract their statement. In effect, the person who has been called out has been cancelled or erased.

People today who identify as 'woke' see themselves as having been awakened to a new set of ideas, value systems and knowledge. They have an increased sense of self-awareness and are unafraid to use their voice for good. There is an ownership and responsibility to continue to develop and grow their understanding of unity in humanity.

There is a relationship between being 'woke' and being an ally. While woke emphasises an individual's understanding of issues, an ally focuses on the importance of taking action to support marginalised groups.

Xenophobia

The fear of a stranger, often coded as a slick alternative term for racism.

Xenophobia is when we fear or distrust people because of their nationality, their lifestyle, their religion, their skin colour. We are not talking about being safe from those who wish to harm us; knowing what fear is helps to protect us from legitimate threats. Our focus is that we learn to be xenophobic because we are fearful of difference.

While fear and xenophobia are related, they are different concepts. Fear is a natural response to danger while xenophobia is an irrational hatred of people who are perceived to be different.

You will be able to spot someone who is xenophobic as their behaviour will include:

1. Being hostile to others by expressing themself through derogatory language;
2. Avoiding interaction with people who are different;
3. Holding extreme nationalistic beliefs in their superiority.

It's worth noting also that xenophobia has a lasting effect. If we close ourselves off to strangers, they will forever remain a stranger – along with people like them – and the cycle gets worse. To push against this, you could commit to making new connections. A good way to do this is to arrange to meet a colleague for coffee after a meeting. You could also send an email to say that you thought their point was interesting and that you would like to discuss it further.

Y

'Yes We Can'

'The creed that sums up the spirit of a people', Barack Obama, 2008 campaign speech.

There is something about how certain people at certain times make statements that become iconic. They are great orators who stir up emotions and inspire us into action. Throughout history there are many examples of great orators. Think of Dr Martin Luther King Jnr's speech, 'I Have a Dream' (1963) or Nelson Mandela's 'I am Prepared to Die' (1964). Obama's speech, 'Yes We Can', was a message of hope.

Today, 'Yes We Can' has become a slogan that has resonated around the world. We see it expressed in music, films and as a form of protest. It has been adopted by many in everyday language and we might say the words to energise ourselves and others.

Z

Zappiness

An emotion felt by Black people when celebrating that is demonstrated by being lively, energetic and happy.

Zappiness is a word that we have coined. It is a state of being and a positive emotion. It can be experienced in proud, positive emotional situations such as at a musical event where there is international attention, praiseworthy group behaviour and a feeling of enhanced status. Zappiness has a particular resonance for Black communities. This is because joy, happiness and ebullience are inherently radical and rebellious when historically Black communities have been denied it.

Like others, Black people have cultural ways in which to express themselves. Some of these cultural ways may come from grandparents, films, stories in books or are contemporary, for example, we learn of them from friends.

Zest

An enthusiasm for life leading to improved mental health.

For some the word zest can refer to at least two things. The first is in a culinary context (the zest of a lemon or orange). The second, and the one we focus on, is about an emotional state. In positive psychology, zest is one of the twenty-four strengths possessed by humanity. As a component of the virtue of courage, zest is defined as living life with a sense of excitement, anticipation and energy; approaching life as an adventure, such that one has motivation in challenging situations or tasks. The other strengths in courage are bravery, honesty and perseverance.

Being treated unfairly because of the colour of your skin is likely to decrease a person's ability to be zestful, and so being Black adds another dimension to being zestful. The opposite of zest is apathy, worry, unhappiness and depression, and this often presents itself as being disinterested, incompetent or lazy. In the workplace more and more organisations use their employment engagement surveys to find out how happy people are at work, and if scores are unfavourable, they examine the data and create strategies to address it. While people might agree that we should bring our best selves to work, if others don't really want you to bring your knowledge of lived experience into team discussions because it is too emotional, then they are not supporting a zestful approach.

The good news is that zest can be learned and practised. Assess what you can really change. Here are three suggestions to start:

1. Personally – get enough sleep, eat well and exercise. Listen to mindful podcasts;
2. In the workplace – find examples of teams where employees are encouraged to put their positive strengths in their email signature (along with their preferred pronouns);
3. Say thank you more often and encourage others to do so.

Resources

BOOKS

Afropean: Notes from Black Europe (2019) by Johny Pitts

Anti Racist Ally – An Introduction to Action and Activism (2020) by Sophie Williams

Black and British: A Forgotten History (2016) by David Olusoga

Black Men in Britain: An Ethnographic Portrait of the Post-Windrush Generation (2019) by Kenny Monrose

Brit(ish): On Race, Identity and Belonging (2018) by Afua Hirsch

Dispatches from the Diaspora: From Nelson Mandela to Black Lives Matters (2022) by Gary Younge

Diversity in the Workplace: Eye-Opening Interviews to Jumpstart Conversations About Identity, Privilege, and Bias (2020) by Bärí A. Williams

Don't Touch My Hair (2019) by Emma Dabiri

How To Be An Antiracist (2019) by Ibram X. Kendi

The Memo: What Women of Color Need to Know to Secure a Seat at the Table (2019) by Minda Harts

The Power of Privilege: How white people can challenge racism (2020) by June Sarpong

Slay In Your Lane: The Black Girl Bible (2018) by Yomi Adegoke & Elizabeth Uviebinené

So You Want To Talk About Race (2018) by Ijeoma Oluo

This is Why I Resist: Don't Define My Black Identity (2021)
by Shola Mos-Shogbamimu

*Uncomfortable Conversations with a Black Boy: Racism,
Injustice, and How You Can Be a Changemaker* (2021)
by Emmanuel Acho

Why I Am No Longer Talking to White People About Race (2017)
by Reni Eddo-Lodge

ARTICLES

'Cultural competence and cultural humility: A critical reflection on
key cultural diversity concepts' by R. Danso in *Journal of Social
Work* 18.4

'Implicit Social Cognition: Attitudes, Self-Esteem and Stereotypes'
by Anthony G. Greenwald and R. Banaji Mhazarin in
Psychological Review 1995, Vol.102, No.1, pp. 4-27

PODCASTS/ TALKS/ VIDEOS

Colour Brave by Mellody Hobson, https://www.pwc.com/us/en/
about-us/colorbrave.html

How I'm fighting bias in algorithms, TED talk (2017)
by Joy Buolamwini, https://www.ted.com/talks/
joy_buolamwini_how_i_m_fighting_bias_in_algorithms

Let's Talk About Race in the Workplace by Marshall E-Learning
Consultancy, https://marshallelearning.com/e-learning-courses/
lets-talk-about-race-in-the-workplace/

Vision and Justice: Race, Technology, and Algorithmic Bias (2019),
with Joy Buolamwini, Latanya Sweeney, and Darren Walker at
the Radcliffe Institute, Harvard University, https://www.youtube.
com/watch?v=Y6fUc5_whX8

WEBSITES

Afropean – www.afropean.com

Black History Month – www.blackhistorymonth.org.uk

Harvard University Implicit Association Test – https://implicit.harvard.edu/implicit/takeatest.html

I-Cubed Group – www.i-cubedgroup.co.uk

Acknowledgements

Thanks to Dulcie Pryslopski for her creative insights, Dr Kenny Monrose for being a font of all knowledge and Anna Argenio, our editor, for her constructive comments and encouragement.